Praise for *It Takes What It Takes*

"In this book, you'll learn how to use the same concepts I employ on the field in your life."
— Russell Wilson, Seattle Seahawks quarterback and Super Bowl champion

"Everyone must check out my dear friend, legend, and mental coach Trevor Moawad's new book *It Takes What It Takes*. The Daily Vitamin you need."
— Ciara

"To be a champion on and off the field, it takes not only being in peak physical condition but being in top mental condition as well. I have had the good fortune to work with Trevor for a number of years and he is very trustworthy and one of the top individuals in this space. This book will give you a front-row seat to some of the powerful concepts our coaches and players have had unique access to."
— Jimbo Fisher, head football coach, Texas A&M University

"I have had the pleasure of working with Trevor for the past eighteen years, and if gold medals were awarded for commitment, honesty, and integrity, Trevor would certainly be a triple gold medalist. His tireless dedication to the athletes he works with is without equal. I have learned from Trevor and I depend on him for valuable advice in my own work."
— Michael Johnson, four-time Olympic gold medalist and president of Michael Johnson Performance

"The field of sport psychology and its discipline of mental conditioning has grown dramatically within the past fifteen years, and Trevor Moawad has been at the center of its impact. I have been a colleague of his for eighteen years, and Trevor has not only navigated this field with some of the best college football programs, elite athletes, military, and top corporations, but he has dominated it. This book is a must read for players, coaches, CEOs, and everyone else wanting to improve their mindset!"
— Chad Bohling, New York Yankees director of mental conditioning and Dallas Cowboys mental conditioning consultant

"Trevor Moawad has a unique understanding of the truth about human behavior, and this book provides the tools needed to acquire the outcomes that we desire. He has the gift of making incredibly complicated realities simple so that as a head coach in an NCAA Power 5 Conference, I can take decisive action today that will help me get what I want. There are no shortcuts. Trev helps to provide me with perspective on my current position in time and provides practical thought options that energize me to move forward boldly. This book gives you a front seat into what he has done for me, Nick Saban, Jimbo Fisher, Kirby Smart, and countless others for the last eighteen years."
—Mel Tucker, head football coach, University of Colorado

"I train my body relentlessly in order to be prepared for competition. Working with Trevor on having a neutral mind has given me the same tools mentally and allowed me to build an invincible mind."
—Marcus Stroman, pitcher, New York Mets

"The mind is so incredibly powerful, and Trevor does a great job of teaching how we can apply his lessons about neutral thinking to improve our performance in our everyday lives. It's not only critical to understand what you need to do to achieve your personal and professional goals but also what behaviors you need to eliminate. Regardless of your vocation, Trevor can help you change the way you think, talk, and live."
—Lawrence Frank, president of basketball operations, LA Clippers

"Trevor has had the unique ability to establish relevance with some of the most powerful sport leaders, athletes, and programs in the world. He not only built these relationships, but has sustained them, and continually found ways to add value."
—George Pyne, founder and CEO of Bruin Sports Capital

"Trevor is at the top of his game when it comes to mental conditioning. His advice is invaluable on and off the field, in the classroom as well as in the boardroom. This book is a must read for anyone looking to step up their game and realize their true potential."
—Christopher Brearton, chief operating officer of MGM Studios and board member of USA Swimming

IT TAKES
WHAT
IT TAKES

IT TAKES
WHAT
IT TAKES

How to Think Neutrally *and* Gain Control *of* Your Life

TREVOR MOAWAD

with ANDY STAPLES

HarperOne
An Imprint of HarperCollins*Publishers*

HarperOne

HarperCollins books may be purchased for educational, business, or sales promotional use. For information, please email the Special Markets Department at SPsales@harpercollins.com.

FIRST EDITION

Designed by Terry McGrath

Library of Congress Cataloging-in-Publication Data

Names: Moawad, Trevor, author. | Staples, Andy, author.
Title: It takes what it takes : how to think neutrally and gain control of your life / Trevor Moawad with Andy Staples.
Description: First edition. | New York, NY : HarperOne, [2020] | Summary: "From a top mental conditioning coach who has transformed the lives and careers of elite athletes, Fortune 500 CEOs, and military personnel, battle-tested strategies that will give readers tools to manage negativity and achieve any goal"— Provided by publisher.
Identifiers: LCCN 2019029436 (print) | LCCN 2019029437 (ebook) | ISBN 9780062947123 (hardback) | ISBN 9780062947147 (ebook)
Subjects: LCSH: Attitude (Psychology) | Adjustment (Psychology) | Thought and thinking. | Success.
Classification: LCC BF327 .M63 2020 (print) | LCC BF327 (ebook) | DDC 158—dc23
LC record available at https://lccn.loc.gov/2019029436
LC ebook record available at https://lccn.loc.gov/2019029437

---

20 21 22 23 24 LSC 10 9 8 7 6 5 4 3 2 1

To anyone who wants to get better

Contents

Foreword   *xi*

Prologue   *1*

1 It Takes Neutral Thinking   *21*

2 It Takes a Plan   *45*

3 It Takes Hard Choices   *69*

4 It Takes a Verbal Governor   *87*

5 It Takes a Negativity Diet   *99*

6 It Takes an Ad Campaign in Your Brain   *115*

7 It Takes Visualizing   *135*

8 It Takes Self-Awareness   *153*

9 It Takes Pressure   *179*

10 It Takes Leadership   *195*

11 It Takes Role Models   *221*

12 It Takes What It Takes   *229*

Acknowledgments   *237*

Notes   *247*

IT TAKES
WHAT
IT TAKES

Foreword

By Russell Wilson

B efore every game, I work with my coaches and
teammates to make sure we have the best offensive
plan possible. After we install those schemes, I meet with
Trevor. He's the man who helps me create my mental plan,
which is just as essential to winning as any other part of my
preparation. Essentially, Trevor helps me unlock the power
of my brain so that I can deliver a peak performance.

Trevor's lessons are powerful, and they can be used
on and off the field—in basically any endeavor you can
imagine. They shouldn't be limited to elite athletes.
Everyone can benefit from what he teaches. In this book,
you'll learn how to use the same concepts I employ on the
field in your life.

My mental training started when I arrived in Bradenton,
Florida, early in 2012 to train for the NFL draft at IMG

Academy. The first person my agent, Mark Rodgers, introduced me to was Trevor. The academy had coaches who would help me run faster and throw more accurately, but Trevor was the guy I really wanted to get to know. He was the director of performance at IMG, and it would be his job to help train my brain. "One of the things I really want to do is spend a lot of time with you," I told Trevor. "My mind is one of my best attributes, but I want to enhance it."

Physically, I had all the talent. I had put up great numbers at NC State and at Wisconsin. But everybody said that at five foot ten, I was too small to be a starting quarterback in the NFL. So when I met with teams before the draft, I wanted my mental talent to jump off the page. How I approach the game. How I approach life. How I was able to face adversity and overcome. Trevor would prepare me for those meetings.

We spent a lot of hours together. I'd be out training, but as soon as that was over I did mental conditioning work. Trevor and I clicked in so many ways because of his passion for being successful. But we also came together around his passion for having a limitless mind. (Which, not coincidentally, is the name of the company we'd create together.) We really grew on each other. I told him about some of my favorite players. The thing that stood out about those players—the guys like Drew Brees, Michael Jordan, and Derek Jeter—was how those guys processed things and overcame things. Trevor saw a lot of similarities between me and Drew Brees, another QB who had trained at the academy eleven years earlier. A lot of people had considered Drew too small to start at QB in the NFL. None of those people will be saying that when Drew gets inducted into the Hall of Fame after he retires. I wanted to learn what he learned, and Trevor guided me through it. We did a lot of drills to increase focus, and we talked about a lot of scenarios. How would you respond? How would you react to this? It really prepared me. This work was something I did with my dad a lot. It transferred to Trevor, and he became a huge part of the mental side of my sport and my life.

We kept working together after the Seahawks drafted me. Trevor has been with me for a Super Bowl win, a Super Bowl loss, and nearly every other football scenario you can imagine. We talk almost every day during the season. We try to meet every Thursday to talk in depth. He'll fly to meet me wherever I am. It's a major part of game preparation for me. What am I saying to myself? What am I saying to my teammates? What language am I using? How am I impacting myself? How am I impacting others? How am I being my best self every time I step on the field? It's critical to have a fundamental mental plan. Anything we go through in life is a new map to a new destination. What's the story we want to tell? How are we going to write that story? Trevor helps me choose the best words.

Sports is very similar to business. You're there to win in business, and you're there to win in sports. Sports also is also very similar to fatherhood. In family situations, you're there to provide and to help everyone else be successful. As a quarterback, my goal is to make the other ten guys better. How can I put us in the best position possible to be successful every Sunday? That's a tall task. But we've been able to translate tough moments into great moments. Moments of clarity. Moments of growth. Exceptional moments. That comes down to the language that we speak and the things that we say. It's also our body language. It's the same thing if you're a CEO or a young person trying to get his first job. At the end of the day, the things we say, the body language we give off, and the people we're surrounded by affect our internal and external growth and possibilities. That's everything. Trevor and I try to capture that every time we talk, and then I try to live it.

In our ten years together, we've learned time and again that neutral thinking is everything. The reality is that positive thinking can work, but we're not sure if it works every time. I'm definitely a positive person. But if you're down 16–0 in the NFC Championship Game, there's not much to be positive about. The one thing we know that definitely works is negative thinking. And it always works negatively. Negative thinking is never going to get you anywhere. Neutral thinking is going to the truth. Where are we at? What situation are we in? How are we going to execute? It's a little like the way the Navy SEALs think. "What's our mission? How are we going to win?" The same thing works in sports. How can we be detail oriented and focused on the task at hand? Some people may call it keeping an even keel, but I think it's deeper than that. I always want to remain neutral.

After a while, thinking neutrally becomes natural. I don't believe in failure. I believe in growth moments—if we use them correctly. As we go through the highs and lows of life, we can utilize our experiences from the past. It can become a habitual thing. It's like riding a bike. The greatest athletes in the world, the greatest business leaders in the world, they have that as a habit because they've worked on it. I'm working on the mental side almost every day. I'm constantly working on being the best version of myself. I'm never there, so I keep working. We use all our moments to help build up for our next great moment.

The mind is a critical piece of all of our greatest moments. In the sports world, we train our muscles to be strong so that we can be at our best when the critical moment arrives. I also choose to train my mind. If we never train it, then it won't be the best it can possibly be. Usain Bolt came out of the womb fast. He trained to be the fastest. I came out of the womb blessed with big hands and an ability to throw a football. But if I hadn't trained that ability, I wouldn't be as good as I am today. The same thing applies to our minds. The difference is that everyone uses their minds no matter what they do for a living. What is the capacity of our minds if we train them? That's why Trevor and I created Limitless Minds, to help train minds in corporations, on teams, and in schools.

You'll learn many of those lessons in this book. I'm a firm believer in that training. It can change our self-esteem. It can change our relationships. It can change our view of success and how we obtain it. It can change communities. It can change the world.

Prologue

Everything went according to plan that Sunday in December 2015. My client Russell Wilson completed twenty-one of thirty passes for 249 yards and three touchdowns and led the Seattle Seahawks to a 30–13 win against the Cleveland Browns. That win clinched the Seahawks' fourth consecutive playoff berth. The playoffs had seemed far away when the team started abysmally at 2–4, but now they were headed into the postseason on a high note.

I was in a suite above CenturyLink Field with Russell's mom and brother and his future wife, Ciara. They celebrated and laughed and smiled and snapped photos to make sure they remembered every detail. I remember every detail, but I don't need pictures. The image burned into my mind? My wife, Solange, sitting amid all that joy looking absolutely defeated.

My job when I work with Russell is to help prepare him for whatever comes next—be it on the field or in the postgame press conference. But Russell had everything under control. I didn't. From the start that day, Solange was really uncomfortable. She had started to withdraw. In truth, I had noticed a disconnect beginning in 2013. We had met in the Charlotte airport in 2005 when our flights were delayed by a hurricane. I lived in Bradenton, Florida. She lived in nearby Sarasota. She was a former model who at the time worked at an animal clinic, so after I got home I borrowed my friend's dog and made an appointment so I'd have an excuse to see her. Six months later, we were engaged. We married in 2007, but as demand had grown for my services as a mental conditioning coach, I had spent less and less time at home. I hadn't paid enough attention.

"I don't want to be here," she told me in the suite. "I don't want to make a scene. This is killing me. This is not the life I want to live. This is not what I want to be doing. I want to leave right now."

We both knew something was terribly wrong, but we didn't have The Big Talk yet. We spent Christmas with my family in Seattle. Then Solange went back to our home in Arizona, and I went to my next engagement—helping the Florida State football team prepare for the Peach Bowl against Houston. That game was miserable. Starting quarterback Sean Maguire broke his foot, but tried to gut it out. Houston jumped on us and rolled to a 38–24 win.

Afterward, I had to fly home and then drive to meet the Arizona State football team, which was about to play West Virginia in the Cactus Bowl.

I walked into the house, and Solange was sitting in the living room in her pajamas. I knew something was wrong. I started walking up the stairs, because I had only a few minutes to grab new clothes before I had to leave again. "You said you'd make some time to talk to me," she said. I turned back down the stairs. "I have some time now," I said. (Which was sort of true.)

When I got back down the stairs, her eyes had already started welling with tears. "I can't do this anymore," she said. "I love you, but I can't do this. I know you are trying, and you take such great care of me, but this is not the life I wanted." There are things that get said between people in a marriage that you know you can debate. That you can stand up to. Then there are the statements you can't counter. I realize it sounds as if I should have seen this coming, but not being with Solange for the rest of my life had never crossed my mind before.

Ever.

But in that moment, I knew our marriage was over.

Emotions are hard for me. It could be a product of constantly navigating through others' challenges for my job, or it could just be that emotions are hard for me. I held her close and stayed very quiet. "You feeling this way wasn't part of the deal either of us signed up for," I said. "I can see that no words will solve this. Just give me some time to process." Then I kissed her on the forehead.

I sound pretty composed considering the gravity of this situation, right? That's probably because the way I was raised and the stuff I'd been preaching at work combined to put me on autopilot through those next few minutes. I went upstairs and threw on a suit. Then I got in the car and began driving to meet the Arizona State football team. I had a presentation to make, and then I had to speak to individual players and coaches. Ten minutes into the drive, it fully hit me.

My marriage was over.

It felt as if the frame of my Jeep were closing in around me. Every muscle in my body clenched. I couldn't breathe. I pulled over near DC Ranch in Scottsdale and stared out the window. Who could I call? I grabbed my phone and texted Florida State football coach Jimbo Fisher, who had just finalized a divorce from his wife of twenty-two years. If anyone would understand, he would.

"Do you have a quick five, Coach?" I texted. He said yes, so I called, and he answered immediately.

Jimbo: *What's up, buddy?*
Me: *My wife just told me . . .*

I couldn't finish the sentence.

Jimbo: *Trev, just breathe. I'm here for you.*
Me: *She just said . . . she said . . . our marriage is over.*

Almost two years earlier, I had watched in a locker room beneath the Rose Bowl as Jimbo had—in the span of four minutes—convinced a team that was trailing Auburn 21–10 at halftime of the national title contest that the game was under control and that the Seminoles could win. His calmness and his stirring message in those four minutes changed everything for that team. Florida State did come back and win that game 34–31. Jimbo raised a Waterford Crystal football, and I realized on that night exactly why he gets paid millions of dollars to coach. Now, on the other end of the phone, he was giving me my own halftime speech when things looked the darkest.

He talked. I cried. I hadn't cried like that since my father was diagnosed with stage four multiple myeloma in 1999. "There will be time to navigate this, Trev," Jimbo said. "And I know you. You will get through it, and so will she."

I took a deep breath. This was the most challenging moment of my life, I realized. I knew it wasn't just a moment either.

There were many months and years of struggle ahead. But Jimbo's confidence in me made me remember: I already possessed the tools to navigate the time ahead, even under the most brutally difficult circumstances. I'm the best in the country at what I do. NFL players, NBA teams, Major League Baseball teams, and elite college football programs all seek my advice to gain a mental edge. I help teach their leaders to lead. I help them create the behaviors that lead to the outcomes they desire. I give them tools they can use when adversity strikes, and I help them replicate success once they've achieved it. This works whether you're an elite athlete, a teacher, an accountant, or a mental conditioning consultant. I knew all this, but I needed to start living my own advice *personally* instead of only professionally. All the techniques I'd been teaching the football, baseball, soccer, and tennis players I'd worked with over the years could help me face this potentially crushing life event. I wasn't playing in the Super Bowl like Russell had or coaching in the national title game like Jimbo had, but wasn't this the biggest event in *my* life? Why not apply the same strategies?

That's why I wrote this book. You don't need to be an elite athlete to train your mind like one. You simply need to have challenges that must be overcome. And guess what? You're human. So you absolutely face challenges every day at work and in your personal life. Maybe you were passed over for a promotion. Maybe you're trying to go to school to better yourself while working and aren't sure how to squeeze everything into the twenty-four hours in a day. Maybe you have a shitty boss and don't know how to manage your interactions. Maybe you've just had a child and you're struggling to adapt to all the extra work at home. Maybe your spouse just told you it's over. Once you've finished this book, you'll be equipped with the same tools I'd give a team seeking a title. You'll learn that champions don't think negatively or positively; they think neutrally. You'll learn that champions behave as if they have no choice. You'll learn that champions make detailed plans. You'll learn that champions visualize what they want. You'll learn that champions lead themselves before they lead others.

You can do this. By cracking open this book, you've already shown you want to grow and change. So let's do it. It takes discipline. It takes sacrifice. It takes time. It takes what it takes.

My Journey

How did I get into this? In a way, I was raised for it. My father, Bob, was a high-school-basketball-coach-turned-self-help-pioneer who was sought by school districts and Fortune 500 companies to teach people how to make themselves better. He owned Edge Learning Institute, which provided motivational speakers and seminars to businesses and schools. He also created the Increasing Human Effectiveness program, which is still in use in the business world more than ten years after his death. For two years in the 1990s, he served as the president of the National Association for Self Esteem. He played the saxophone, the ukulele, and the piano. As a speaker, he could tell tales that left thousands of people hanging on his every word. In fact, you may have seen some of my dad's words before—possibly on a poster or on one of those quote-of-the-day sites. Here are a few samples:

- Most people don't aim too high and miss. They aim too low and hit.

- Attitudes are contagious. Do you want people around you to catch yours?

- You can't make footprints in the sands of time if you're sitting on your butt. And who wants to make buttprints in the sands of time?

- Who wants to be average? Average is that place in the middle. It's the best of the worst or the worst of the best.

My mother calls me my dad's science project. My brother, Bob Jr., who is seven years older than me, had a more "normal" upbringing. Looking back now, it feels as if my parents raised me in a way they hoped would prove the efficacy of my dad's ideas. (Which, if you haven't noticed, I believe are very effective.) When I was very young, I'd go to sleep with a tape from the Nightingale-Conant motivational

company playing white noise that was supposed to have
embedded subliminal messages that would help build my
self-esteem. When I got a little older, they switched to You're
Nature's Greatest Miracle, a series of cassettes my father had
put out in 1980. Side one of the first tape included the song
"Gettin' Rid of Stinkin' Thinkin'." Before bed, my mom,
my dad, or both would come in and we'd recite a set of
affirmations. They sounded something like this:

- I take setbacks as temporary and I bounce back quickly.

- I love myself unconditionally.

- Yes I can, regardless of the circumstances
  I'm faced with.

- I'm a great student and I do great work.

My dad's belief was that "the human mind is the fastest,
coolest, most compact and efficient computer ever produced
in large quantities by unskilled labor." He believed that
we could enter data into our minds that would help set an
expectation the way you set a thermostat. My dad's career
was almost like a second sibling to me. It's connected to me,
but it's a different person. It was more a way of life than a
job for him.

As I got older, I transitioned from recited affirmations to a
set of note cards. On the front, I'd write something I valued.

Maybe it was school, working hard, my family, or success. On the back, I'd write the behaviors that I'd need to use to have success in the area named on the front. I'd review the cards on my way to school. I'd review them at school during lunch. I'd review them at night. I didn't buck against my dad's philosophies. I embraced them. Starting in seventh grade, I would read a quote of the week to the whole school. Everyone knew the family I was from. I never ran from it. I remember playing basketball in high school against Steilacoom High near Tacoma. Steilacoom taught one of my dad's programs in its health classes, so all the students knew who I was. As I stood at the free-throw line dribbling, the crowd chanted "PO-TEN-TIAL" at me. I could only laugh.

Even though my parents worked hard to instill these principles in me, I don't think I truly learned to live them as a teenager. I didn't understand this until the end of my third semester at Occidental College. I played soccer and basketball at Oxy, a small liberal arts school in Los Angeles. My sophomore year, I also pledged Sigma Alpha Epsilon. The pledge semester included something called Hell Week, which turned hellish for me for reasons that had nothing to do with the older brothers in the fraternity. By the second day, I felt horrible. I went to my room in Norris Hall and slept for ten hours. As I rolled over, it felt as if someone had shoved needles through my back. A few teammates and fraternity brothers came up to check on me, and we found my temperature had spiked beyond 104

degrees. I was taken to Huntington Memorial Hospital in
Pasadena, and I told the guys I'd get back to them when
I was done. I thought it would be a quick visit. Instead, I
wound up surrounded by a lot of different doctors. At the
end of the day I was brought into a back room. An older
doctor came in. He had an incredible bedside manner, and
that helped tremendously as he delivered a diagnosis and
an educated guess. "Son, you have done a number on your
immune system," he said. "It's in a very difficult place. You
have a disease called shingles on top of a number of other
challenges. With your white blood cell counts what they
are, we believe you may have a form of cancer."

The room seemed incredibly still. I was so young. I had
no concept of what he was saying. I had been on a date
earlier that year and seen a Michael Keaton movie called
My Life. In the film, Keaton's character gets diagnosed with
kidney cancer, and he immediately begins making videos
so the baby his wife is about to have will have access to
everything he's learned. I couldn't imagine being that guy.
I had no wife. I had no baby. I had never given serious
thought to my mortality. But while I was confused, I wasn't
ignorant. I knew this wasn't good news.

The doctor let me process the information. Then he told
me to go home to Seattle to my regular doctors, because
more testing was required for any definitive diagnosis. "At
eighteen, this is tough news for parents," he said. "Call
them and ask to come home. Sit them down and take them

through this and start the process of trying to both get healthy and find out specifically what we are dealing with." I went back to Oxy, withdrew from the frat, and called my parents and said I needed to come home that night. I booked the last flight to Seattle from the Burbank airport.

When I arrived at Sea-Tac Airport around 11 p.m., I headed to baggage claim nineteen to pick up my luggage. Then I walked outside to find my ride. I didn't see my dad's car. I tried calling home collect—only Gordon Gekko had a cell phone at this point—but no one answered. (My parents had fallen asleep and couldn't hear the phone ringing.) I had no money for a cab. Uber was a generation away. So I walked back inside and sat against a wall.

As I sat there, everything hit me in waves.

Wave 1: *Why the FUCK is this happening?*

Wave 2: *I've barely lived. I haven't had sex or partied or succeeded at any elite level. I complained about playing time in sports. I've literally done nothing . . .*

Wave 3: *My college life up until now is a huge disappointment. In my first quarter I borrowed a friend's history paper and wrote half a paper myself and used half of his and got caught. I got hauled before the academic board. They flunked me in that class and told me any further academic missteps would result in expulsion. Margin for error? Gone. I also got a D+ in a language course simply by* *not applying myself or showing up to the labs. My combined GPA for my first quarter was a 1.67. I had never behaved this way before. Probably because at home there was a guy who wouldn't let me behave that way.*

Wave 4: *Everything my dad has been telling me feels real right now.*

By the time I finally woke up someone at my house and secured a ride, nearly five hours had passed. I made some powerful decisions in that time. College exposed me to a constant comparison battle. How did I measure up to other people? My life those previous semesters wasn't about who I was. It was about who I thought I wasn't. I hadn't become a star in basketball or soccer. I didn't have entire sororities chasing me down the street like I was a Beatle. I thought this was what I was supposed to become in college, and I had been ripping myself internally for not becoming this person I imagined I'd be. But this moment helped me see that the more important questions I needed to ask were How do I measure up to me? Am I using the gifts that I have?

Short answer: Not well. And I wasn't.

I didn't want to go down that road anymore. Some learn in advance of adversity. A lot of us learn through it. In later months and years, I came to look on my revelation that night as my psychological birthday.

I took time away from college to figure out my health situation. It took a while for my immune system to rebound enough for doctors to get any sort of accurate results. Eventually they realized I didn't have cancer. My colon was wrecked, however, and they initially diagnosed me with Crohn's disease. Then pancolitis. Then just plain ulcerative colitis. When they finally put me on the correct medicine, it took only about a week before I looked like nothing had ever happened. I eventually returned to school and to sports. But something had changed inside me. *The health scare, in retrospect, was necessary to get me to reboot. It made me realize I needed to return to behaviors that had helped me excel in high school. The behaviors Bob Moawad had taught me by lesson and by example.*

Once I got healthy, physically and mentally, my grades rose. I began loving sports again. College became what it is supposed to be—a bridge to adulthood. After graduation, I worked as a US history teacher at John Marshall High School in the Los Feliz neighborhood of Los Angeles. I figured working for an urban public school would teach me the skills I needed to teach anywhere. I just never dreamed some of the skills I learned would eventually help me teach Georgia and Alabama football players how to think as they prepared to play. I liked working with the kids, and I was lucky enough to get paired with Sharon Pitkin, the student teacher supervisor no one wanted to have. She was the toughest. She was a disciplinarian. She said I had a real aptitude for teaching and she was not going to let me slack at all. She taught me how to teach. Delivery never was a problem for me. But she taught me how to prepare lessons and how to identify when to move forward and when to slow down to ensure my students stayed engaged. Once I understood that framework, I could roll.

As much as I liked educating, something felt off for me. I didn't feel like a history teacher. Eventually, I knew, that would become a problem. I left Marshall after two years and moved across the country with my then girlfriend. I settled into a job teaching history and coaching soccer at North Broward Prep High in Coconut Creek, Florida. It still didn't feel right, but it led me to the job I was meant to do. A coaching clinic took me across the state to a school in Bradenton founded by tennis guru Nick Bollettieri. Originally designed to train tennis players and golfers, the school had been bought by IMG, which added programs for hockey, baseball, soccer, and basketball. The place was basically Hogwarts for athletes, and some of the best in the world trained there. During the clinic, I watched a presentation by Jeff Troesch, who ran the mental performance unit for the academies. After that hour, I knew what I wanted to do with my life.

I spoke to Jeff briefly afterward and learned he had also grown up in Seattle. He knew who my dad was. In the next few months, I left Jeff voice mails. I wrote letters. I did anything I could to let Jeff know I wanted to break into his business. He eventually agreed to meet with me, and my dad flew in for the meeting. Jeff offered me an internship for the summer of 1999. It was unpaid with no housing. I didn't care. I just wanted a chance. When I arrived, I realized the other interns were there to get college credit. I was there to start a new profession.

How did I get noticed? I could sell. When kids came to the academy for camps, they got a certain amount of physical and mental training with their tuition. But parents could buy more. I would call parents of kids who were headed to camp. They would ask what was already included. I'd tell them the kids would get two lectures on Tuesday and Thursday and they'd be great lectures. Then I'd let them know we had some individualized programs. We'd put the kids through a battery of tests. We'd put them on the court and videotape them. We'd do the same thing we do for Tommy Haas or Anna Kournikova. Then we'd analyze the video and send it back home with them.

The other interns hated selling those packages. I smoked them. We had a list of bullet points we needed to hit to explain the details of the packages, but I always added something extra. I had a chart of area codes. I would look at the parents' phone number and try to reference something local that everyone would know. Anything to establish a little bit of a connection. (This could backfire now, because in the mobile phone era people don't always live in the area code of their phone number. But everyone just had landlines then.) I wanted to control the narrative as best I could. I'd frame it this way: Simply put, you are spending $2,000 to send your son or daughter to one of IMG's academies for a week. Don't you want to feel like you eked out every gain possible? This last $350 helps insure and protect the $2,000 investment. I'd ask them about the influence they thought the mind had on their son's or daughter's performance. Did they have access to sport psychology or mental conditioning support in their town? The answer, of course, would be no. This would reinforce the critical mission I'd set out for them (protect your investment). Through this process I not only learned a lot about what worked and didn't work, but I also found out that I was uniquely equipped to talk about mental conditioning due to my own engineering. Jimbo would say what makes me unique is that I grew up speaking this language my whole life. Those phone calls were my *Karate Kid* "wax on, wax off" moment. All that unique training became clear as I realized I was fluent in a language I didn't even know I could speak—mindset.

My phone prowess endeared me to Chad Bohling, who worked in Jeff's office. I got offered a job that fall, and I was ready to accept when my dad asked me a question. "Son, didn't you already sign your contract to teach?" he said. "In our family, we honor our contracts." I had, and he was right. So I taught one more year, but I also volunteered at Chris Evert's tennis academy to remind myself of what I really wanted to do.

The next year, I took a job at IMG. My life was designed to get to Bradenton. The academy was my pro sport. It was my NFL. I was either going to make it or fail. I was going to be in this competitive landscape where if I was going to be good at what I did, I was really going to excel. I tried to soak in everything I could. When a group that included LaDainian Tomlinson, Drew Brees, and Steve Hutchinson trained for the NFL draft on campus, I sat in on their sessions. The US under-17 soccer program trained on campus, and I volunteered to videotape their games and meet with their players. I didn't get paid for that, but I would later when US Soccer hired me to work with the next set of under-17 players.

This led to work with some of the best athletes in the world. It led to the Jacksonville Jaguars and Fred Taylor. It led to Nick Saban hiring me to work with the Miami Dolphins and then Alabama. It allowed me to meet Russell Wilson, who would become a client and one of my best friends.

It hasn't been easy. Not all coaches are as open to new ideas as Nick Saban is. The most common statement I heard early in my career was "You've got four minutes." That's how long some coach or general manager or athlete would give me to explain exactly what the hell a mental conditioning consultant did.

How do you build trust with the best coaches and athletes in the world? The same way you sell a mental training package to a parent over the phone. You find the value proposition, wherever it ends up being. There is no set way. There is no "Please have him show up at my office at this time." I work on their time in whatever environment they choose. My "office" has been a broom closet, the west officials' bathroom in Jacksonville, the field, some incredible IMAX-looking team meeting rooms, hotel rooms, patio decks, hikes, weight rooms, staff rooms, an NFL boardroom, and, of course, a lot of middle seats flying 35,000 feet over America.

No matter where I work, the same truth keeps emerging. Neutral thinking is the key to unlocking a set of behaviors that can turn also-rans into champions and champions into legends. But you don't need to be an elite athlete to take advantage. Keep reading and find out how thinking like a Super Bowl–winning quarterback can help you win in all aspects of your life.

1

It Takes Neutral Thinking

Sports is a business. Teams are no different from Google, Microsoft, Safeway, or any other company—except the environment is more cutthroat. The best earn promotion, and those who can't maintain the standard are let go. You win or you get fired. This is the world I work in. These are the standards.

As of this writing, Seattle Seahawks quarterback Russell Wilson is the highest-paid player in NFL history. To put it in business terms, he keeps getting promoted. He's also my client and one of my closest friends. His story merits a Disney trilogy. Undersize. Doubted. Accomplished. No quarterback in NFL history had more wins in his first eight seasons, and Russell is one of the chosen few to be a consumer-facing brand in a league worth $14 billion. Russ is elite. He is everything I've taught for eighteen years manifested in a single athlete.

In 2014, Russ had just reached the pinnacle of his profession. He had won the Super Bowl in his second NFL season. His trajectory pointed straight up. But the past season doesn't always create momentum for the next. The months following the Super Bowl win against the Broncos had been especially trying for him. In April 2014 he filed for divorce from the high school sweetheart he'd married in 2012. His team, my hometown Seahawks, would start the season with massive expectations but struggle to a 3–3 record before bouncing back to win nine of their last ten regular-season games. Then the Seahawks beat the Carolina Panthers in their first playoff game to set up a QB duel between Russell and Aaron Rodgers as Seattle and Green Bay faced off for a spot in the Super Bowl.

To put it bluntly, Russell played one of the worst fifty-five minutes of his young football career. With 5:13 remaining and his team down 19–7, he fired a pass over the middle toward Jermaine Kearse. The ball ricocheted off Kearse's hands and into the waiting arms of Packers safety Morgan Burnett. It was Russell's fourth interception of the game. He'd thrown a good ball, but it wound up getting caught by the other team. It definitely wasn't Russell's day.

As all this was happening, I was in Memphis. I was working with the NBA's Grizzlies, and they had a game later that night. I watched the Seattle game on a TV in the team dining room, living and dying with each throw Russell made. As I watched the meltdown, I thought back to one of the first meetings Russ and I had in 2012. I'd told him about a core truth that I had learned working with the football teams at Alabama and Florida State. Each play has a history and life of its own. It's important. It matters. You are responsible for it. But it has nothing to do with what happens next.

Russell's agent, Mark Rodgers, had called me at halftime from a suite in the stadium in Seattle. "The great thing," I reminded Mark, "is you know Russ will play all sixty minutes regardless of what preceded it. Good or bad." Mark agreed. Russell is what's known as a competitive thinker. He's never out of the fight in his mind.

Down 19–7, Russ hadn't gone into the tank. You could tell when the Seahawks next got the ball back. "We can still win this game!" Russell yelled. "Let's go! Four minutes and fifty seconds!"

Why hadn't Russell given up? Why did he treat the next play as if the previous ones didn't matter? Because he stayed neutral.

Neutral thinking is a high-performance strategy that emphasizes judgment-free thinking, especially in crises and pressure situations. It is the cornerstone of what I teach the athletes and teams that employ me. The thing about neutral thinking that resonates with so many elite athletes, most of whom are deeply skeptical of any self-help, is that it's real. It's true. It acknowledges that the past is irrevocable, that it can't be changed with mantras or platitudes.

Neutral thinking shuns all attempts at illusion or outright self-delusion, which are often the foundation of other motivational systems. Neutral thinking strips away the bull and the biases, both external and internal.

There are more biases in this world than there are fruit flies and gnats—combined. They're everywhere you look, many of them buzzing around your own psyche right now. Confirmation bias, selection bias, negativity bias, recency bias, gender bias, optimism bias, pessimism bias—it's hard to clearly perceive reality when your subconscious is busily prejudging it.

Don't feel bad. It's not just you. Bias is an inherent part of nature, among humans *and* animals. (Yes, animals are shown to have cognitive blind spots too.) Much of the animate world—heck, maybe much of the *inanimate* world, according to some philosophers—filters and alters reality.

Even your naked eyes, scanning this page, aren't giving you the unvarnished truth. They're taking two flat images and sending them separately to your brain, which is then fusing and remaking those images into one three-dimensional image, while also independently choosing which colors to use in painting that image. Your eyes are telling a biased story to your brain, which then tells you another biased story, and each stop along the way in this optical-neuronal game of telephone gets you a little further away from reality.

The most dangerous bias when discussing performance is our innate privileging of the past. We elevate the past. We give it too much importance. We serve the past when we should be giving it a wide berth.

Russell knew that from years of practice. In that moment in Seattle, he could see the four interceptions for what they were. They had happened, but they didn't have to affect the next four minutes and fifty seconds. He wouldn't let them. He leaned on truth-based thinking that evaluates reality in real time. He knew there are three distinct states: what has happened, what is happening, and what will happen. The interceptions had happened. What was happening was the dominant Seattle defense got the ball back for Russell and the offense. What would happen was he would make the necessary adjustments to play better going forward and one good series would give his team a chance to win. The truth was they were down only twelve points. That was the reality he knew in that moment. That was Russell being neutral. I could see it in his body language as I was pacing back and forth with the Grizzlies players. (I'm not so great at staying neutral when my clients are thousands of miles away.)

Russell led two incredible touchdown drives. But as the
reporters in the press box rewrote the Seahawks' obituary,
Aaron Freaking Rodgers would lead a field goal drive
to knot the score at 22 at the end of regulation. After
examining Green Bay's defensive tendencies through
the first sixty minutes, Russell had some thoughts as
he approached offensive coordinator Darrell Bevell in
overtime. "You know what would be good?" Russell asked.
"That check." Russell referred to an audible—a play change
made at the line of scrimmage—he thought would work if
the Packers dropped extra defenders down near the line
of scrimmage when Seattle used a tight formation that
suggested a running play. The check would leave receiver
Jermaine Kearse—yes, the same guy from interception
number four—matched up one-on-one with a defensive back
who wouldn't have the usual help from a safety roaming
the deep third of the field. Bevell agreed. "Yeah," he said.
"Be ready." Then Russell doubled down. "We're going to win
the game on it," he told Bevell. Just before the Seahawks'
offense took the field again, Russell approached his
teammates. "Hey," he said. "Be ready for the check." Russell
didn't think about the four interceptions he'd thrown.
Those were over. He didn't think about Kearse's drop that
caused the fourth interception. He'd thrown enough passes
to Kearse to know that had been an anomaly. Russell didn't
think about the tumult in his life the previous year. He
went to the truth of knowing how he had prepared and
knowing the tendencies he'd seen in the Packers' defense in
the games he'd watched on video and in the four quarters

he'd just played. He didn't tell himself he was the second coming of Joe Montana. He also didn't doubt that a guy who had already thrown so many picks could win this game.

When the Seahawks huddled on the field to start overtime, Russell addressed the group. "We were meant for this, men," he said. "We were meant for this." Later, on first-and-10 from the Packers' 35-yard line, Russell saw the look he'd predicted. "CHECK 50!" he screamed. "CHECK 50!" As he'd predicted, Kearse was matched up one-on-one. Russell dropped a throw into Kearse's hands just as Kearse crossed the goal line. Four interceptions were forgotten. The Seahawks were going to the Super Bowl.

A few months later, Bryant Gumbel interviewed Russell on HBO's *Real Sports*. Gumbel did not mince words. "When you stink up the first half, you don't think about it?" he asked. Russell didn't blink. "No, I don't," he replied. "I think about one play at a time. Let's go. Let's keep it going. Let's keep it going. That's how we all think. That's how we're able to win."[1] How does he do this? It goes back to the idea of three states. What has happened. What is happening. What will happen. Russell never pretends that—good or bad—the past didn't happen. If he was focused on positive thinking, then he'd have to do that to some extent. Sports has a scoreboard that makes your reality incredibly clear. Since the time Russell was twenty-one, we've always discussed the idea that we are "defined in the present." This is the idea behind the "one play at a time" cliché, which became a cliché because taking things one play at a time has proven to be an effective course of action. It's anchored in the concept that each moment has a history and life of its own.

Neutral doesn't mean you have to be a robot. Russell was as animated during that game as he's ever been on a football field. But that didn't stop him from remaining neutral and focusing on his influence on the next behavior. It also allowed for a bigger release after the Seahawks won. "That game and the emotion you saw was bigger than just a game," Russell told Gumbel. "It was about my life. It was about the past year of my life and the ups and downs of it."[2] That quote has always moved me, just like his tears. His reaction at the end of the game showed what emotions were bubbling beneath the surface for Russell that day. How did he keep them from overwhelming him? By staying neutral, which has the dual effect of allowing you to move on from what has just happened as well as controlling the emotions swirling inside you. An emotion is merely another form of bias. It's your brain trying to sneak those biases into your thinking. But Russell, who by that point had become great at thinking neutrally, knew he had to strip away those biases to get to the undistorted truth.

Had Russell let his emotions insert those biases, he might have thought like this: "Maybe this just isn't my year. I'm getting divorced. We started the season poorly. I've thrown four picks today. Maybe next year will be better." Instead, he focused only on what was true: "There are four minutes and fifty seconds left. We are down twelve. We need to score twice. Their defense is showing the same looks we saw on video, looks that expose some vulnerability."

A neutral mindset allowed Russell to ignore the swelling emotions. Once the game was over, Russell could release them. Winning in any competitive event means you take something from someone else who wants exactly what it is you took. There are no trust funds in the sports world. Victory can't be bought. It must be earned, and when you earn it, the feeling is amazing. It's even more than that when life has beat the shit out of you—as it can do to the best of us. That year was a battle for Russell. It was up and down, but he remained neutral and reached another Super Bowl. He understands he doesn't have choices if he wants to be a star quarterback in the NFL. He has a narrow path, and the only way to stay on that path is to stay neutral. To be aware of the past. Grounded in the present. In control of the next behavior.

USC quarterback JT Daniels talked a lot about this tendency in his postgame news conferences in 2018. "Accepting the past as a real event is powerful," he told me when we met up in Manhattan Beach after the season. "It also frees you when you understand the next event is independent of that past—and can actually be different."

I couldn't have said it better myself.

I started working with JT when he was a fifteen-year-old prospect in Santa Ana, California. He was a quick learner and an eager student, his locker filled with half a dozen notebooks. I was amazed and gratified by how intensely this kid embraced neutral thinking.

So I wasn't all that surprised when he became a five-star recruit, one of the top high schoolers in the country. He had talent to burn, of course, but I like to think neutral thinking helped him maximize that talent. And I think he'd agree. He's said publicly that he tried positive thinking before I came along. It wasn't bad; it just didn't empower him like neutral thinking does.

After we'd been working together for about two years, JT packed his bags for USC, where he became only the second true freshman ever to start week one for the Trojans. He had butterflies before that first start, of course. So did I. And not everything broke his way—beginning with his pregame prep. His phone died, so he couldn't listen to his music, his special playlists, to calm himself, as he always does before a game.

Then, in the early going, he stumbled a few times. But he regained his composure and overall notched a solid performance. Afterward, he explained to the media that he tried "to be as neutral as I can with my thinking." I heard him say that and puffed out my chest like a very proud papa.

Week two was a debacle, one of the worst games of JT's life. Stanford's defense suffocated USC. JT completed only sixteen of thirty-four passes and threw two interceptions. His team lost 17–3. He didn't hide from it or offer excuses. He also didn't make it more than it was. He kept his eyes forward. What can I do to get better, fast? Two weeks later against Washington State he played one of the finest games of his career. Three touchdowns, no turnovers, tons of poise.

JT put it to me beautifully one afternoon in Manhattan Beach after the season. "As a starting quarterback, you've got to be able to go to the truth." Yes, yes, yes. Neutral thinking lets you go to the truth. And stay there. And live there.

A mistake at work, in a marriage, as a parent, in a big-time college football game—it's real. It happened. I don't believe in pretending it didn't. I don't believe in telling yourself it's anything other than what it is. But I also don't believe in enlarging it, in viewing it as the end of the world, which is what so many of us do. What happened happened. Okay. Fine. What happens next has nothing to do with that.

What happens next will be determined solely by what you do next, and what you do next will be the absolute right thing, I promise, if you focus on that thing and that thing alone.

The past isn't predictive. The past isn't prologue. If you can absorb and embrace that belief, everything can change.

Your brain, however, doesn't want to do any such thing. Your brain is a perpetual motion machine. It's used to being in drive or reverse. Downshifting your brain into neutral takes practice. But once you get the hang of it, once you develop the skill to shift your thoughts into neutral, you can go to the truth on a dime. You can deal with the facts at hand. Where are we? What can we do next? How can we best do it? You'll feel more calm, more aware of the situation as it unfolds moment to moment. And the athlete—or employee, or spouse, or parent—who's more calm and more aware generally succeeds.

Some might call it mindfulness. It certainly overlaps with aspects of mindfulness. But neutral thinking is more than simply being mindful. It's a quick pivot step toward swift, decisive, stunning action.

Mindfulness doesn't care if you win.

I do.

The idea of neutral stirred somewhere deep within me in my youth. It would expand a bit as I studied Taoism and the idea of balance in college. It would become much more prominent as a facilitator of mental conditioning concepts in the battleground of the sports world. Players knew that negative thinking would hurt them, but man, they struggled with positive thinking as the only alternative— just like I did. The actual truth is not negative or positive when you remove judgment from it. It simply is. Neutral is the harmony between two extremes, negative and positive. Neutral thinkers remain aware of the situation as it changes from moment to moment. We give ourselves the opportunity to learn from every situation, even if the outcome is not optimal at that specific time. The next behavior remains consistently in our control.

I met with a director of professional development at Goldman Sachs after being part of the keynote presentation for their annual CFO conference in 2018. He asked me what white papers I had to explain the efficacy of neutral thinking. I told him what I share openly with others: research studies back up this approach, but I haven't conducted studies in a lab. I've lived the approach on fields and in team meeting rooms, both winning and losing. I've been to college football national championship games with three teams, and I've lived this approach. I've never been signed to more than a one-year contract with a team or an athlete, ever. This has forced me to develop real-time solution-based processes that can help players and coaches right now, and neutral thinking is a significant part of this process.

The moment I came to believe that we might have a movement was January 1, 2018, in the locker room at the Rose Bowl in Pasadena. Imagine entering a sixty-minute event in your field of expertise and having someone take a belt to every part of your body for the first thirty minutes before giving you a fifteen-minute break. This was what the first half of the Rose Bowl felt like for all of us associated with the Georgia football team that year. Oklahoma quarterback Baker Mayfield showed why he had just won the Heisman Trophy. It felt like every decision he made was perfect. It also felt like he had a wide-open receiver on every play. The Sooners averaged nine yards a play against a defense that had been great all year, and we went into the locker room down 31–17.

We were not inferior to Oklahoma. Far from it. But we had clearly played the inferior half of football. Think about that statement. How many times does that happen to us over the course of an event in our own lives? You may know that you are better than you just performed, but you also know you just performed like shit. It's in this moment that positive thinking becomes a challenging leap for even the best of thinkers. How do I separate what just happened from what will happen when I am the same person or we are the same team or I work for the same organization? To me, it has to work just like a car works. Ever try to go directly from driving in reverse to driving forward without pausing? Your engine doesn't like it, and neither did your tires when you laid down all that rubber. Your brain can't handle that transition either. The correct order is reverse to neutral, then neutral to forward.

At halftime in the Rose Bowl that year, we had to shift into neutral before we could go forward. The good news was that Georgia was the first client for whom I'd integrated a full platform that focused on neutral thinking. The idea of less negative defeating more positive had lived with us at both Alabama and Florida State and at Fort Bragg. Neutral had been a smaller piece of the curriculum for those teams. Georgia coach Kirby Smart had been the defensive coordinator on those Alabama teams, and he hired me when he took over as the Bulldogs' head coach in 2016. By then I had realized the power of neutral. So for a full eighteen months we integrated this idea that I illustrated using examples from sports, business, and even space travel. And now, in the biggest moment of Smart's young head coaching career, he was fluent in neutral.

He knew it well enough to know he had a problem. "I'm having a very difficult time staying neutral right now, bro," Kirby told me.

Halftime of a college football game doesn't work the way everyone thinks it does. The head coach doesn't gather the team around a dry-erase board and magically diagnose and correct every issue the team suffered from in the first half before delivering a win-one-for-the-Gipper speech. First, players are exhausted. They need a break and a snack. Second, coaches—some of whom have spent the first half in the press box while the rest worked on the sidelines— need to compare notes to formulate the diagnoses and corrections. Players then meet with position coaches in small groups to make these corrections on a micro level.

The head coach gets very little time to discuss the big-picture stuff. So he has to use that time wisely.

Kirby was formulating his message to the team when he told me he was having a difficult time staying neutral. But what he said next proved he'd been paying close attention to all those lessons. "I do know that the first thirty minutes and the last thirty minutes are two distinctly different events," he said. "The key is how we make them look different." He already knew what he needed to do. All he needed from me was a nudge so he could translate that to the players.

This was my fourth Rose Bowl working with a team from the South. Those teams are accustomed to raucous crowds and frenzied pregame situations. So when they got to the more laid-back Rose Bowl—an open, spread-out stadium that plays Bon Jovi instead of DJ Khaled before the game and features an equal split of fans from both teams—they tended to start a little sleepily. I was pretty confident these players would adjust to the atmosphere the way the players in the past had. Kirby's mission was to explain to the players that they didn't need to be better versions of the players they'd been all season to win the game. They simply needed to be the *same* players they'd been all season. They hadn't all played to their own standards in the first half. If they could—especially the players on defense—Georgia could win. Despite the two-touchdown deficit, the offense had actually averaged more yards per play than Oklahoma in the first half. That tracked with what Oklahoma's defense allowed against better opponents. Oklahoma's offense was its usual efficient self. Georgia's defense had been the only group playing out of character. Kirby needed to get that message to his players. If they could revert to the behaviors that had gotten them to the Rose Bowl, they could still win the Rose Bowl—no matter what had happened in the first half.

"Let's play Georgia football like I know you're capable of playing it," Kirby told the team. He didn't need to call down the thunder in his speech to draw more from them. The players understood neutral thinking too. And they knew he was right.

Schematically, Kirby offered a vote of confidence to his secondary by telling those players they'd have less help in coverage because the Bulldogs would send an extra rusher at Mayfield. That also served as a vote of confidence in Georgia's linebackers, who would provide much of the extra heat on Mayfield.

For the remainder of the game, Oklahoma's offense averaged 4.2 yards a play. The defense didn't play spectacularly. It simply returned to its baseline. The genius of Kirby was realizing that his team didn't need anything more than that. It didn't need anything magical. He didn't need to apply additional pressure to his players; he only needed to remind them they were already good enough. And when an oppo-

nent gets almost five fewer yards every snap than they did
in the first half, a fourteen-point deficit doesn't seem insurmountable. Early in the fourth quarter, Georgia led 38–31.

Still, it wasn't over. Midway through the fourth, Oklahoma's
defense made a huge play. Steven Parker recovered a
Sony Michel fumble and returned it forty-six yards for a
touchdown to give Oklahoma a 45–38 lead. Now was the
time for the Georgia offense to stay neutral. The Bulldogs
had been successful most of the day. The facts told
freshman quarterback Jake Fromm and senior backs Nick
Chubb and Michel that they could find the end zone again
if they didn't freak out about the fumble. So they didn't.
And they didn't freak out when Oklahoma's defense forced
a three-and-out on the next possession. They knew their
defense could get them the ball back, and they could be
reasonably certain that Oklahoma's feast-or-famine defense
couldn't win a third consecutive series. And it wouldn't.
Fromm hit Terry Godwin for sixteen yards on third-and-10
from the Oklahoma 23-yard line, and two plays later Chubb
took a direct snap and ran around the right edge for a
2-yard touchdown to force overtime.

The teams traded field goals in the first overtime. In the
second, Georgia linebacker Lorenzo Carter blocked an
Oklahoma field goal attempt. That meant Georgia could
stay conservative on offense and set up a field goal to
win. But Georgia's offensive stars had taken that halftime
message to heart. They knew their normal was better than

the Oklahoma defense's normal. On the Bulldogs' second play of the second overtime, it was Michel's turn to take the direct snap. He whipped around the left side, burst through a hole near the 20-yard line, and sprinted for a 27-yard game-winning touchdown. Georgia was going to play for a national title. It was a huge win for the Bulldogs, but it was an even bigger validation for neutrality.

The Rose Bowl only feels like life-and-death, though. One of my favorite examples of the power of neutral thinking involves three men in an actual life-and-death situation.

Astronauts Jim Lovell, Jack Swigert, and Fred Haise would have died if they hadn't been able to think neutrally after one of their oxygen tanks exploded during the Apollo 13 mission. Their command module crippled, the three of them were left to survive in the lunar landing vehicle designed for two. With help from the folks back in Houston, they dreamed up ways to stretch their water and power supplies to allow them to get back to Earth. They had to plot a new trajectory when the slightest miscalculation could have killed them. When I speak to groups, I play comments from Jim Lovell as he explains how the astronauts and the NASA engineers on the ground thought through the steps required to get the crew back to Earth safely. "There were moments when I didn't know how much consumables we had—whether we could make it back or not," Lovell said at a postflight press conference in 1970. "But in a situation like that, there's only one thing you can do. You just keep going.

You just keep thinking up ways to get more consumables. And so that's exactly what we did."[3]

They didn't worry about the past. They didn't think about the odds. They couldn't afford to do anything but focus on the next steps required to keep themselves alive and to keep them on the correct trajectory back to Earth.

One of the biggest threats after the accident was the rising carbon dioxide level. Every time the astronauts exhaled, the level of carbon dioxide in their tiny capsule rose because the capsule was outfitted with carbon dioxide filters designed for two people over two days and the capsule now contained three astronauts who needed to survive for four days. If the concentration of carbon dioxide in the capsule became too great, it would kill the astronauts. The trio had filter units from the command module, but the command module's filters were square, and the lunar module's filters were round. The team needed to find a way to literally fit a square peg into a round hole. Back in Houston, NASA employees raced the clock to figure out a way to connect the square filters using only materials available in the capsule. Eventually they came up with a plan using bags from the astronauts' liquid-cooled garments (LCGs), a cardboard logbook cover, and duct tape. (Here's a free neutral thought: duct tape remains the answer to almost any problem.) Ground control called up to the module to walk Lovell and Swigert through the process of rigging the filters.

Houston: *Okay. I think the equipment you'll need will be two command module lithium hydroxide canisters, a roll of the gray tape, the two LCGs, because we're going to use the bags from the LCGs, and one—one LM cue card—one of those cardboard cue cards which you will cut off about an inch and a half out from the ring. Now, I think that's all we'll need. Over.*[4]

Had Lovell been only positive in this moment, his response might have sounded like this:

Lovell: *This idea will get us home, and I can't wait to get back to Earth. I know we'll make it now.*

That doesn't sound very realistic, does it? This is a moment where unearned confidence could get the astronauts killed.

Many people conflate realistic thinking with negative thinking. So let's consider what Lovell's response might have sounded like had he been thinking negatively:

Lovell: *Are you insane? Duct tape? Cardboard? All the brightest minds in America and THIS is the best you can come up with? We're all going to die.*

We know that's not a realistic thought or response because we know they did survive. The situation wasn't impossible. In fact, not only was it possible, but it became probable because of the approach they did choose.

Here's how Lovell actually responded:

> **Lovell:** *Okay. That's two lithium hydroxide canisters, one roll of that special gray tape, two LCGs which we're going to use the bags from, one LM cue card and . . .*[5]

He merely confirmed the materials required. Then he and Swigert began asking questions about how everything would fit together. Before long they had rigged the filters, and the carbon dioxide levels began to drop.

That's neutral. Staying in the moment, giving each moment its own history, and reacting to events as they unfold. It takes away emotion and replaces it with behaviors. Instead of asking, "How do I feel?" you should be asking yourself, "What do I do?"

You can develop these skills if you're willing to let go of a few things. Negative, cynical thinking doesn't make you more realistic. It just makes you negative and cynical. Biased thinking doesn't help you either. You need to steer clear of your feelings and make an honest assessment of each situation you face. Don't worry about what you feel. Rely on what you know.

This translates to any workplace. You may despise your boss. But are you going to half-ass an assignment out of spite for the boss? If you do, you might hurt only yourself. Instead, try to look at the assignment neutrally. If you complete the task, you will be successfully doing your job. And if you continuously complete your tasks, the boss will get off your back. You may even get promoted and become his boss. This happens when the truth guides us. When judgment diminishes. We recognize that the present determines the present, and today's behavior is what influences tomorrow's outcomes. Start now.

Thinking neutrally also helps you concentrate when other factors are swirling around in your life. I've had to do that in recent years while dealing with my divorce. Dramatic life events tend to introduce a flood of emotion. Staying neutral can help you manage that emotion. Think about the marathon runner. She has to go 26.2 miles, but is she thinking about the finish line when the race starts? No. That's too daunting. She's thinking about her pacing for the first mile. She's planning out when she wants to grab water or eat a gel pack. Thinking about all 26.2 miles is overwhelming. Thinking about the next few steps is manageable, and it works whether you're running a race, playing for a spot in the Super Bowl, or trying to save your own life in space.

It Takes a Plan

As Solange and I entered the stadium in Glendale, Arizona, hours before the Seattle Seahawks' Super Bowl XLIX game against the New England Patriots, I was relaxed. Russell Wilson's level of preparation creates that feeling. He owns his career. Seattle wasn't my team. But the Seahawks' quarterback is my guy. He was ready. How do I know? I helped him put together his mental plan for that Super Bowl. Russell's agent, Mark Rodgers, who has spent most of his career working with baseball players, had secured former client Mike Hampton's house in Paradise Valley as a place for Russell to get ready. In 2001, Hampton signed an eight-year, $121 million contract with the Colorado Rockies. That kind of money can buy a palace in the desert. On the night before the Super Bowl, I joined Russell, Mark, and Russell's brother, Harrison, there to help Russell prepare his mind for the challenge ahead.

It takes a plan to achieve anything of value. When you plan, you identify an end goal and then chart out neutral behaviors that can help you reach that goal. That may sound overly simplistic, but a lot of people say "I want to do this" without thinking about the behaviors and benchmarks required to reach that goal. Choosing not to plan is actually a plan around not planning. I don't recommend that. You wouldn't drive to a place you've never been without first checking a map or plugging the address into Waze or Google, would you? And what is a set of directions if not a plan? For any big project you take on, you need to map out your route. You need to make a plan. For something huge like the Super Bowl, Russell made multiple plans.

He had the game plan—the specific sets of plays the Seahawks had practiced to use against the Patriots. He and his teammates had spent two weeks building that plan. He also had a mental plan. That's where I came in. I wasn't there to tell him what to check to when the Pats showed Cover 2. My job was to make sure he entered the game in the proper headspace. Mark's idea had been to bring Seattle to Arizona, and part of Russell's pregame routine at home was to meet with me three nights before each game. Because of the scheduling quirks of Super Bowl week, we had to do it the night before the game.

When planning, we start very simply. We identify the goal. In this case, the goal was obvious. Russell wanted to play well and help his team win the Super Bowl. The next part

is where it gets a little tricky. This may require some trial
and error as you set goals in your life, because you'll need
to know yourself well enough to know which method works
best for you. In my experience working with elite athletes,
the ones who haven't experienced great success tend to
want to know what they must do to reach their goals. The
more self-confident athletes want to discuss the factors that
could keep them from reaching their goals. They don't mind
objectively examining the barriers to success. Russell is in
the second group, so he can handle both methods.

We started by giving Russell examples of the times he has
been at his most commanding. We moved to the mansion's
home theater to review a series of situational videos set to
film scores—which shook the room thanks to the surround
sound. Russ sat front and center. As he watched, he allowed
himself to relive incredible moments where he had been
at his best. I had soundtracked part of the video with The
Head and the Heart's "Down in the Valley." A song from
an indie folk band might sound wimpy for a badass QB
prepping for the Super Bowl, but everything has a purpose.
The lyrics tell a story. The sentence "These are the places I
will always go"[1] is repeated four times. I wanted Russell to
see these moments and hear those words and realize he's at
home in those big moments.

In other parts of the videos, he could hear the words he
used and watch the body language he exhibited as he
navigated those situations. Beating mighty Florida State

in Raleigh while playing for NC State. His first preseason camp at Wisconsin after transferring. The fourth-down pass to Jeff Duckworth in the fourth quarter of the Big Ten Championship Game to keep the Badgers' Rose Bowl hopes alive. The NFC Championship Game against San Francisco the previous year and the fourth-and-7 throw to Jermaine Kearse for a 35-yard touchdown to take the lead for good. Winning the Super Bowl against the Broncos the previous season. My questions that would follow were simple.

If it doesn't play out how we want it to tomorrow, what would stop it?

Russell acknowledged that New England's Bill Belichick makes better in-game adjustments than any coach who has ever lived. We discussed what would happen if one of those adjustments stopped the Seahawks' offense. How would Russell react mentally? How would he adjust? We agreed that while schematic tweaks were fine, Russell couldn't stray from the core fundamentals that helped him lead his team to the Super Bowl. No matter what genius moves Belichick made, Russell needed to remember the keys that had lived on his locker in Seattle for the entirety of that season:

- Great fundamentals

- Great balance

- Be engaged

If it plays out exactly as you see it, why would it? How would you influence that?

We discussed starting fast and finishing faster. This wasn't because of the (extremely) slow start in the previous game against the Packers. Russell happens to be better when he starts fast. The comeback against the Packers had been thrilling, but that wasn't his typical game.

His answers to my questions were clear. They were neutral.

I need to execute. To stay engaged. To keep us calm.

"That's who you've been your whole life," Harrison said. Russell kept going.

I need to show my trust in everyone. To trust my reads. To trust my teammates. It will get chaotic. Good and bad. Tom [Brady] will make plays. I need to keep things steady. I will keep things steady. I've seen it. I know it, and I am built for this.

Russell doesn't speak in "ifs" when it comes to his performance. He speaks in "I's." "I do this" versus "If I do this." Why? He knows the impact of his own language on him and on others. "If" implies a choice. He knows there are no choices for leaders in the biggest moments. "If" gives your brain an out. "I" makes a commitment.

That evening wasn't about showcasing Russell's previous successes as much as his ability—over his entire career—to affect the teams he has played on and their capacity to win. Years earlier he had gotten on the phone the nights before National Championship games as I had similar meetings with Alabama quarterback AJ McCarron and Florida State's Jameis Winston. Russell helped reinforce neutral mindsets that would allow AJ and Jameis to execute their roles as pieces of their own teams' puzzles as they played in the biggest games of their lives. Advice from the type of guy Teddy Roosevelt called "the man in the arena" carries a lot of weight to the men about to enter the arena. Russell's counsel helped AJ and Jameis stay neutral, and the fact that the advice worked for those two only reinforced the concept for Russell.

We didn't need to call in for extra advice for Russell that night in Arizona. He had a great game plan and a great mental plan. He was ready.

Twenty hours later Solange and I took our seats next to baseball major leaguer—and former Notre Dame wide receiver—Jeff Samardzija and his wife. The atmosphere was like the biggest SEC games, which tend to be much wilder than NFL games. Seattle's "12th Man" had grown into a pro version of a college fan base. Russ was dialed in amid the pregame chaos. There wasn't a dropped ball in his pregame routine. He was surgical.

After warm-ups, the Seahawks went back to the locker room. They reemerged with The Verve's "Bitter Sweet

Symphony" blasting. Russell jogged onto the field with that unique blend of inner peace and urgency. He had it before I ever met him. People may be surprised that he works to make it even more world-class, but that's the standard and price of sustained excellence.

The Seahawks took a 24–14 lead into the fourth quarter, but when a team has Tom Brady, that team always has a chance. The Patriots scored two touchdowns to go up 28–24, and suddenly Russell had two minutes and two seconds to lead a game-winning drive. In this moment, the Seattle sideline stayed calm. The Seahawks were a fourth-quarter team. A clutch organization. They shone in these moments. Paul Allen was . . . Paul Allen. The team owner had created an incredibly high standard with Microsoft (as the company's cofounder with Bill Gates) and with the Seahawks. Seahawks coach Pete Carroll is a winner, and his team reflects this. I had been around that program enough to see it. They were a collection of winners and, more important, a group organized around great behaviors. After all, winners win only when they behave like people who win. Russell exemplified this. Whether they were facing Jacksonville in a regular-season game or New England in the Super Bowl, this team knew how to finish. These guys were closers.

It amazes people to see how calm Russell is in these moments. He lives for this. This is when he demonstrates the difference between saying "I" and "if." "I am built for this" was on his mind the evening before, and now the moment was here. How many people were watching? There were 70,288 in the stadium. The television audience was the largest in American history. Forget the final episode of *M*A*S*H*. This game averaged 114.4 million viewers. When Russell took his final snap of the game, the audience had peaked at 120.8 million viewers. More than one out of every three humans in this country watched Russell's last play.

As Russell led the Seahawks toward the goal line, the crowd inside the stadium reached absolute frenzy. I couldn't hear anything Solange was saying, and she was inches away from me.

But I knew Russell could thrive in this kind of chaos. When I worked at IMG, we tested him on a device that acted like a souped-up version of the Simon game we played as kids. Colors would flash all around him. He was allowed to hit only the keys that flashed green. His mind focused on green, and that's where his hands would follow.

Russell understood a critical fundamental: the law of substitution. At any given moment our minds can sustain only one thought at a time. One. The thousands of words flying through our brains or screams from outside crowds at riot levels can't overcome that truth. It's universal. My mind doesn't block things out. It simply goes to whatever thought I ask it to go to. My inner voice is loudest. If I don't use it strategically, however, then the words of others or the outside chaos can replace my message to myself. My own words influence me ten times as much as anyone else's. Russell uses that power. We all can. His words in a moment like that? He had stated them the evening before. They live on his locker. On his phone.

- Great fundamentals

- Great balance

- Be engaged

Also, trust. In these moments you go with what you know. You go to the truth. He knew his job was to be steady, and as he took the field for that last drive, that's exactly what he was.

Russell hit Marshawn "Beast Mode" Lynch down the left sideline for a 31-yard gain on the first play of the drive. The Seahawks were already in New England territory. A few plays later, Russ would throw a 33-yard pass to Jermaine Kearse to get the Seahawks to the Patriots' 5-yard line with 1:06 remaining. After a time-out, Russ handed off to Lynch, who bulled his way to the 1-yard line. Why did they call Lynch "Beast Mode"? Because when Lynch entered this mode, tacklers bounced off him. It would take half the defense to bring him down. So as the Seahawks faced second-and-goal at the one to win the Super Bowl, the thousands in the stadium and all those millions watching at home thought the same thought: "They're going to give it to Beast Mode. If he can't get that yard, they'll give it to him again. With three chances from three feet, why would they need to do anything else?"

The Seahawks let the clock drain. If they scored, they didn't want to give Brady any time for a miracle. During that time, the next play came in from offensive coordinator Darrell Bevell. They weren't going to give the ball to Beast Mode. Russell was going to throw it.

Remember how I said everyone thought Seattle would give it to Beast Mode? My numbers might have been a little off. There may have been three people who thought the Seahawks would try something different: Patriots coach Bill Belichick, Patriots defensive coordinator Matt Patricia, and Patriots cornerback Malcolm Butler.

When Russell took the snap with twenty-six seconds remaining, Butler broke immediately toward receiver Ricardo Lockette. Had Butler hesitated for a split second, Lockette would have caught Russ's pass and the Seahawks would have won the Super Bowl. Instead, Butler arrived just before the ball did. He snatched it as he bounced off Lockette. Then he fell forward as the rest of the Patriots celebrated. They had just clinched a Super Bowl win, and Russell had just thrown the pass that lost the Super Bowl, with the largest television audience in American history watching and judging.

And many of those millions were merciless. They blamed Bevell for calling the play. They blamed Carroll for not overruling Bevell and calling for a handoff. But most of all, they blamed Russ for throwing the pick.

Three years later, Russell and I would go over this play and its aftermath with former Oklahoma State quarterback Mason Rudolph for our ESPN show *QB2QB*. "Right here, in this moment, you realize that if you're going to go for something, you're going to have some heartbreak," Russell told Rudolph as the interception played out on a nearby wall. "But if you're not willing to go there, you're never going to get there." In other words, you have to be willing to be the goat—the old, negative meaning of the word my generation grew up with—if you ever want a chance to be the G.O.A.T. (what younger generations call the greatest of all time).

Minutes after throwing the interception, Russell had to face the cameras and explain what the hell happened. As he walked to the press conference, he thought over what he would say—how he would frame this moment. Even now, less than half an hour after an enormous public professional failure, Russell stayed neutral. "Our team, everybody, we fought all season just to be able to accomplish a tremendous goal," Russell recalled thinking during the walk. "The one thing I've always realized is this. Whether it's me holding up the trophy or not being able to hold up the trophy—either way—I wasn't ever going to let that define my career."

Some of us will remember the brutal press conference Carolina Panthers quarterback Cam Newton gave after losing Super Bowl L to the Broncos. His answers were short and clipped. After a few terse responses, he just walked away. Later Newton admitted in an interview with *Ebony* that he could have handled the situation better. "Who is anyone to tell me, 'Man, it's just an interview'? You haven't been in that situation," Newton told the magazine. "You didn't have millions of people watching you. Your heart wasn't pumping [with] the embarrassment or the anxiety of the stress of dealing with that type of game. I just wasn't ready to talk. Was I mad? Hell, yeah! But there could have been a better way to control it, and that's why I think having more time would have helped."[2]

Russell had the same amount of time a year earlier. His loss had come on a gut punch on his final play, not as the result of getting battered for an entire game. He had been in an arguably tougher situation and had answered every question.

Russell told Mason and me about how losing his father would always be harder than losing any game. "I'll never forget the moment he passed away," Russell told us as he explained his mindset during the press conference. "The hardest moment of my life, hands down. When he passed away, I said this to myself: the sun's still going to come up in the morning."

Then Russell explained how he could learn something from the loss. "You keep your head up," he said. "I'm never down. I can never be down. I'm grateful for the opportunities that I get. You have to take things like a man. You have to take things with strength and understanding. And even though it's not easy to understand in the moment, you have to know that there's going to be clarity someday. There's going to be clarity and understanding."

This comparison is not meant to disparage Cam Newton. It's meant to show the difference between negative and neutral thinking. Having to explain to a bunch of strangers why you just lost the Super Bowl is an incredibly difficult task. Few people are equipped to handle it properly. Russell was, because Russell has always known how to stay neutral.

That mindset also helped Russell take the correct next steps.

Because while it's important to make a plan, the best realize that sometimes their first plan gets blown to smithereens and they have to respond by making a new plan. Russell and the Seahawks had a great plan for that Super Bowl. Had they won it, Russell could have used the same plan he'd used the previous off-season. Who could have argued with the result? But Belichick, Brady, and the Patriots had a better plan for that Super Bowl. Now Russell needed a better off-season plan than the one he had the year before to overcome the mental fallout from the game. From The Play. From the avalanche that followed.

At 6 a.m. ten days after the Super Bowl, a text message from Russell popped up on my phone:

> **It's time to hit the reset button.**
> **Let's make this the best off-season yet.**

My response?

> **On it. Agreed.**
> **It's completely in our control. 24 hours.**
> **The BEST is Ahead RW.**

I've never viewed myself as a sports psychologist. The best teams and organizations aren't calling anyone often, in my experience, and when they do, they're not looking to start that relationship with me in an office. I had significant doubts about my ability to grow at IMG or EXOS in that role, and I wanted to grow. I wanted relevance. I wanted to make money. To do that, I had clear "choices." I would develop additional skills and take more important positions that would include overseeing all training at IMG and, later, running the professional sports business at EXOS—the unquestioned best professional sports training facilities in the world. To do this, I learned every element of training and how the pieces come together. I began building behavior platforms with many of the best brands and experts to launch young pros and keep the best ones on top. Body, mind, recovery, social skills, media, and humanity. It all mattered. Nick Bollettieri gave me a front-row seat to the best of the best at twenty-six years old. I sat in on meetings with or about Serena Williams, Maria Sharapova, Eli Manning, Tony Romo, Jozy Altidore, US Soccer, and growing the academy business as a whole. I was surrounded by the best agents, the best federations, dynamic families, and the best experts across IMG's incredible platform. Seven years in, Bollettieri and others had given me the keys to oversee all of the athletic development at the world's toughest playground. No "mental coach" had been given this opportunity before. It was a year into my marriage, and the new professional focus probably got my personal relationship headed down the wrong road. I hate knowing that reality now, but I loved the opportunity I was given. I took it. This is what *I* was built for. People are surprised to find out that I'm not a sports fan. I'm a fan of growth. I believe in people. Wherever that journey starts for them, I can see what they will become when weaponized with the right behaviors. I see it in eleven-year-olds. I see it in sixty-year-olds. I saw it in the football complex at Alabama. I saw it with my first U-18 girls club team. And all of them would get my best.

It all can be trained. Everything. Every single fucking thing can improve. We aren't meant to be stagnant. I help develop people. In that, I developed myself so I could become the top guy doing it. Russell knew that. I had earned the right for him to ask me to help develop this plan. And it would be both my privilege and my responsibility to take his incredible aptitude and put it in the best daily situations to make his next moment—the off-season following The Play— elite so his next season could be epic. The past is the past. Russ knew that. People aren't defined by the past unless they choose to live there. He didn't. Neither did I. The people of Seattle, however, did. They couldn't help it. They love their team, and their hearts were broken. Even if they meant well, daily reminders of that interception weren't going to help. So we needed to get the fuck out of there.

That's where Russell and I started developing the next plan. We had identified the goal: conduct an off-season program so great that Russell would come back better than the QB who had just led his team to consecutive Super Bowls. Now we needed to build the steps that would help Russell be that QB when he reported to the Seahawks' organized team activities (OTAs) in April.

We realized atmosphere matters more than most people realize. I explained why Russell couldn't stay in Seattle. But where could he go? The previous summer, Russ and his manager had anchored down in Manhattan Beach. That was a different situation, however. Then, he had just won the Super Bowl. His on-field success was at an all-time high. Endorsements. National television. The world had seen what I saw in the first ten minutes after we met in 2012. But along with all the excitement, he had been dealing with a life challenge—the end of a marriage. That off-season was built to manage everything that came with that as well as with the on-field success. It was focused on getting back to another Super Bowl, which is exactly what the Seahawks did. This off-season would be about getting back to the basics that had provided the foundation for those two Super Bowl trips.

Manhattan Beach is wonderful. I wanted somewhere where the sun shone in blue skies nearly every day. Weather affects mood, and we needed to reset our mood. No dreary skies for us. Manhattan Beach fit the bill, but it's also a hive of activity. We wanted sunny and boring, because Russell needed to focus on the task at hand. Manhattan Beach is just too interesting. So I looked two counties south. I thought San Diego would be the right place because of the volume of blue-sky days, the weather, the serenity, a great collection of top-flight training centers—we had an NFL quarterback who needed to work out, after all—and easy access to LA. Within thirty-six hours—twelve hours too long for Russell—we had rented a 3,000-square-foot home in a very quiet suburb of San Diego. Thirteen days after the Super Bowl and he was already on to the next season. Solange flew in to finalize the interiors of the house, and we snuck up to La Costa in Carlsbad for a night. "Only Russell would pick a community where the average age is seventy!" she said.

The first arrivals in San Diego were Prince and Naomi, Russell's two beloved Great Danes. Russell's bags followed. Russ himself would be coming down later that day. In four

hours we secured a fence for the dogs, loaded the house
with food, got the bags to Russell's room, set up a massage
center in a guest room, and prepped the pool for Russell's
stretch and cooldown later that night. Do these tasks sound
menial given my job title? For years people would tell my
former partner Chad Bohling and me, "That's not your job,
bro." We always knew the reality: getting shit done *is* the
job. Whatever it took. Both of us could get anything done.
Anywhere. Any time.

As the private airport's gate opened, I drove toward the
sunset. The plane was dead center of the intimate facility.
It felt like a scene from *Top Gun*.

Russ walked off the plane.

"Love you, bro," he said. "Thanks for doing this."

"Wouldn't miss it, RW," I said. "The best is ahead."

"The best is ahead," he replied.

The journey forward had begun. It had really begun
with his postgame press conference thirteen days earlier.
Choice? There are no choices as to how a leader handles
a moment like that if he wants to move himself and his
team forward.

"Pete [Carroll] says it's his fault," I said. "Do you agree?"

"I put the blame on me," Russell said. "The ball was in my hands. I threw it."

That was the mental part. Owning it. He'd held the trophy the year before. He'd shoulder the other side of it now. Derek Jeter—Russell's favorite athlete—said what Russell was now living: to be able to hit the game-winning home run, you have to be willing to strike out in the same batter's box. That translates to football pretty easily. To have a chance to throw the touchdown pass that wins the Super Bowl, you have to be willing to throw the interception that loses the Super Bowl. Those two things live in the same moment.

With atmosphere covered, we moved on to the next piece of the plan. Russell had a specific physical objective: he wanted to get faster. The next morning, we visited some of the best facilities in California. Together we would decide who would be trusted to help him achieve his goal to run a 4.4-second 40-yard dash. To not be caught by anyone. That was his mission. This part of the plan would be built around that.

Confidence is the belief that you can do what is demanded. This is why I've never bought into the idea that the mind is anything more than 5 to 10 percent of the equation. I spent as much time overseeing all elements of training at IMG as I did working in the psychological space, and it is clear to me that if you don't have the physiology and skill set to achieve something, no amount of will can overcome that. But that small percentage makes a world of difference. When you're elite, you need to be holistic. You need to have a plan for everything. You need to train it all. Russell's success in 2015 would have a mental component, of course, and we had a strong plan for that. His confidence, however, would be built on his physical preparation. That would be driven by commitment, strategy, and the right process.

Ryan Flaherty, who now serves as Nike's VP of performance, would earn Russell's trust to help guide him through the process. And Ryan was perfect.

His facility was filled with top-level athletes. Arizona Cardinals quarterback Carson Palmer. Future second-overall NFL draft pick Marcus Mariota. Olympians. Ryan passed the eye test. You don't get these athletes by accident. But several trainers in California had that. What separated Ryan out in Russell's mind was that he had elite intelligence and a great sense of humor. In advance of the meeting, he had studied Russell's movement patterns and stride mechanics and had them clearly mapped out on his flat screen in his office. He explained how a path existed to get where Russ wanted to go and the commitment from Russ that would be required. Ryan, it turned out, also had a plan. He and Russell each understood that commitment goes two ways. Both were in.

There's a significant difference between wanting a great off-season and committing to one. One of the

true challenges of choosing sports as a career is the
physiological requirements to function. Your job, in many
cases, is far more body than mind. Your mind may steer
the ship, but the ship still needs to be built for rough seas.
No Boston Whalers survive in the NBA, NFL, or MLB.
It takes a battleship. I've worked in all those leagues as
a strategic consultant in mental conditioning. And in
all those years around some of the very best in sports—
coaches and athletes—a few things became clear:

- It's what you do, not how you feel, that gets things
  done. We can do our way into feeling the way we
  need to. It's hard to feel our way into achieving a
  damn thing.

- We all want things, and there's value to that; want
  is a precursor to motivation. But want is an idea.
  Commitment is execution.

Over the course of this journey there would be times when
I swear I could see Russell replaying The Play in his head.
I never knew for sure, and he'd never talk about it. He
wouldn't give it that power. He had analyzed the decision
after the game in film study with his Seahawk teammates.
He gave it the appropriate attention; then he moved forward
to this off-season. Words—good or bad—would give the past
unnecessary influence. He was educated in this area well
before experiencing Super Bowl success and Super Bowl
heartbreak. That education was a weapon for him. It helped

him manage success (because he knows how to sustain it) and adversity (because he knows how to move past it).

As the off-season started, I usually arrived at Russell's house early in the morning. The uplifting sounds of Hillsong UNITED—a Christian rock band from Australia that specializes in beautiful harmonies—always filled the house. I learned that Russell's music is an important part of how he sets his tone. The chords were melodic, the message was powerful, and it was all intentional. I'd later integrate what worked for Russ into my own life. The same music with the same goals.

That off-season Ryan Flaherty would introduce Russell to chef Andrea Witton, a great part of his team who would become his full-time nutrition and food guru. She'd have prepared meals available or would cook for Russell, his manager, and myself. My videographer, Jon Schultz (a young Spielberg), found literally every fourth-quarter comeback in Russell's career going back to high school. And there were a lot of them. Each morning we'd cue up a comeback from a designated game at various times in his life.

Every play would include predetermined music with TV audio as Russ would lead his team back. This is what I know—if you are what you do, then when you don't you aren't. I wanted to remind Russell of historical precedent. Who he was based on, what he had done, as a means of reminding him what he *could* and *would* do next. My dad called this imprinting. In the 1980s he'd have NASA leaders, IBM executives, educators, and athletes write down specific memories of strong performances on note cards and put a plan in place to review and relive them. He understood that words trigger pictures, which impact emotions, which lead to performances. He'd teach me this process as flick back/ flick up—flick back to a past moment, and then flick up and apply that past behavior to a future moment.

The latest research says that members of Generation Y— the population I primarily work with—prefer to learn visually. I had three fully focused staff members who had taken imprinting to the next level. Many people, in my opinion and experience, have evolved into visual learners regardless of their age. Technology has reconditioned us this way. Strong visual stories create the conditions for powerful follow-up with dialogue or discussion. The best way to educate is to combine learning with functional entertainment—to "edutain." The athletic world's truth is not about making the presenter look or seem intelligent. It's about making information consumable, relevant, and immediately applicable.

The audience I was with (Russell) embraced this kind of stimulus. So we bypassed the writing phase and went right to the picture, the memory, the emotion, the behavior, and then discussed its connection to the next moment. That was the psychological breakfast that accompanied the chef's protein-based one. Both would have value for Russell in this training cycle. He knew it. So it became part of his process. The truth had the ability to outweigh any external narrative. The truth was that Russell Wilson was one of the best quarterbacks in football. Win or lose. He wasn't defined by one event. He and the Seahawks had made a plan for the Super Bowl, but some of the greatest to ever play and coach had made a better plan. So Russell had to make a better off-season plan.

As of this writing, Russell hasn't made it back to the Super Bowl. Reaching the Super Bowl is an enormous challenge and not something you do alone. (Ask Dan Marino, Warren Moon, or Dan Fouts.) But Russell did have his best statistical season in 2015. He threw a career-high thirty-four touchdown passes and averaged a career-high 8.3 yards an attempt.

It was almost as if he'd planned it.

3

It Takes Hard Choices

I got hired by the Memphis Grizzlies in 2014. It was my first foray into basketball, and it gave me the chance to work with some amazing athletes. Perhaps the most amazing was Vince Carter, who had joined the team that year for his seventeenth NBA season. As of this writing, he's still playing in the NBA at age forty-two. That kind of longevity can only be the product of great choices. Sure, Vince has superior genes. All you have to do is watch video of that 360 in the 2000 Slam Dunk Contest to know that. But everyone who makes it to the NBA has superior genes. Not many people make it in the league for ten years. Barely anyone plays into his forties.

Vince played his college ball at North Carolina, but he grew up in Daytona Beach, Florida, as a huge Florida State football fan. I worked with the Seminoles during the same period I worked with the Grizzlies, so Vince and I bonded talking about Jimbo Fisher's team. I also worked with Alabama at the time, and early in 2015 the Crimson Tide were dealing with a few high-profile off-field issues. The most recent was a DUI charge for cornerback Geno Smith. During a conversation about those issues, Vince asked me what percentage of players at the top level of college football expect to play in the NFL. I estimated about 70 percent. To Vince, this seemed crazy. Anyone with a basic grasp of math can see that even the very best college football programs see only about 10 percent of their players find success in the NFL. Vince was amazed that so many players could have such a goal while behaving in ways so counter to what it would take to actually achieve that goal.

Vince had built his career on making choices that led to behaviors that helped him reach his goal: keep performing at a high level in the NBA for as long as possible. Over the years, he has revealed a lot of these choices. Some of them are simple decisions any of us could make in our own lives.

He stretches more often. Anyone can do that. He drinks more water. He told *GQ* in 2017 that he can't remember the last time he drank soda. He cut back on fried foods. He avoids the pizza and wings that sometimes get delivered to NBA locker rooms for postgame meals. He never goes to sleep immediately after eating, so he can give his body time to digest.[1] We all can make those choices, and we'd probably all be better off for them.

Some of Vince's choices are unique to Vince. For example, he told SB Nation he chooses not to dunk so much anymore. This isn't because age has rendered him incapable. He can still throw it down better than half the players in the NBA. But Vince understands his knees have only so many dunks in them, so he doesn't crush the rim when a layup will suffice. Also, a powerful dunk does have an immediate impact on him now. It takes a second or so to recover, and that second could give two points to the other team because it delays Vince from getting back on defense.

Vince also works out after games now. While most of the other players are on their way home—or, if they're making different choices, to the club—Vince is in the gym. He focuses on his core in these workouts, because keeping that strong keeps everything else from breaking down.

During that 2015 conversation, I asked Vince a question: Is choice an illusion? Of course, he said. There was no way he'd still be in the NBA in his late thirties if he'd done everything he wanted to do. He did what was demanded. "So it takes what it takes?" I asked. "Exactly," he said.

The next day I was scheduled to drive from Memphis to Tuscaloosa to meet with the Alabama football team. I couldn't get Vince's story out of my head. So I started typing, and when I was done I had the words I'd present to Nick Saban and his team.

"The Illusion of Choice"

— *A lot of times we feel as if we have choices to make about where we want to go and WHAT IT TAKES to get there.*

— *The REALITY is that what it takes to succeed is not REALLY a choice.*

— *WE GET tired of talking about it.*

— *I get tired of talking about it.*

— *I know we all do—but we are going to talk about it until we RESOLVE it.*

— *ANYONE who runs a marathon will tell you that miles twenty to twenty-six are the hardest.*

— *AND ANYONE who quits running at mile twenty-two will tell you that they immediately felt better—and IT'S TRUE. But days later when they read about the people who finished ahead of them—who kept running—they will have instant regret.*

— *MY point is that THE ONLY CHOICE YOU HAD was to come to this school.*

— *ONCE you chose that, you said, "I'M GOING TO BE ELITE."*

— If that's true, then the FORMULA is the FORMULA.

— YEARS from now when they look back at this ALABAMA team, all that WILL BE LEFT is WHAT WE DID.

— NOT what WE COULD HAVE DONE, if only this or this happened.

— IF we are ELITE—IF we are a team who BELIEVES BIG—then WE DON'T have a "choice" about how we finish this SPRING.

— NONE.

— THIS game rewards people who DO IT RIGHT.

— THIS game has demands—YOU DO them and succeed or YOU DON'T do them and you struggle. THERE is no middle area.

— MY point is we don't "have a choice" about how we are going to do things if we are going to STAY TRUE to the goals WE ALL made to start this year.

I presented these thoughts to the coaching staff first and later to the players. The content wasn't fundamentally different from what I had taught previously, but the conversation with Vince had crystallized the message. There is no choice. It takes what it takes. This resonated with the coaches because it was a simple, unimpeachable way to say something they're always trying to get across to their players. None of us had said it this way before. This is probably my biggest strength and the best advantage of growing up as Bob Moawad's son. My dad was always trying to adjust his phrasing to make it resonate with the largest audience, and he knew when he'd found words that hit the target. This phrasing hit the mark. I could see it in the players' eyes. I could see it in the coaches' eyes. They understood. I see that same recognition every time I present to a new group and explain the illusion of choice. "Of all the things you teach, Trev, nothing hit me between the eyes like the illusion of choice," MGM Studios COO Chris Brearton told me. "It so clearly is true, and yet we all compete against our own choices every day." Deep down, we all know our choices ultimately determine our behaviors and those behaviors ultimately determine our outcomes.

That doesn't make choosing correctly any easier in our own lives.

Making bad choices is the lifeblood of average. It feeds it. It consumes it. It protects it. Choice is a competitor—as much as any tangible opponent you or any team will face. In fact, it's the ultimate competitor. It taunts you. It will lie to you. Take choice out of your way, and it's like pulling the fitness band off Usain Bolt. The Velcro snaps, and watch his ass disappear. Choice is an illusion. Choice is Keyser Freaking Söze.

This may sound crazy, especially in an age where many people are bombarded by options. The music we listen to. The shows we watch. The time we wake up. The food we eat. The people we associate with. The way we prepare. The effort we give. The effort we don't give. But do we have the luxury of choice if excellence is what we aspire to?

Before we go further, you need to understand how I'm defining the difference between options and choices. Options are what I call choices that don't have real consequences. If you want to watch a TV show, are you clicking on a broadcast network, a cable network, Netflix, or Hulu? If you're hungry, do you get pizza, pad thai, chicken tikka masala, or sushi? And do you cook, go to a restaurant, or have Postmates or Uber Eats bring it to your lazy butt? These are all options.

But choices, even small choices, are the decisions that matter. Some probably sound familiar:

- Do I go to sleep at a reasonable hour or do I finish season four of *Breaking Bad*?

- Do I drink this Jack and Coke, which will inevitably lead to another and give me a wicked hangover that will absolutely keep me from being productive until 1 p.m. tomorrow? Or do I order water so I'll be ready to roll at 7 a.m.?

- Do I spend time with my kids, or do I play *Halo* for a few more hours?

- Do I start work on this presentation that isn't due for three weeks, or do I cruise Facebook to see what my friends are up to?

You know the correct answers to all those questions. Everyone does. That doesn't mean they're easy to answer correctly in the moment. If you care about results, however, there are relatively few paths that will lead where you want to go, and the sooner you understand that, the sooner you can start putting yourself on those paths. When I started working with the Alabama football team, I would hold a bag of Doritos in one hand and an apple in the other. "Do you really need a nutritionist to tell you which one of these things is better for you?" I asked the players. This seems like such a simple thing, but if you've ever stared into the bottom of an empty chip bag and wondered how it got that way so fast, then you know it's incredibly difficult for most people to make that particular correct choice, much less the series of correct choices required to win a gold medal or a Super Bowl or lead the company in sales.

Are you willing to make the sacrifices necessary to be successful in your life? You don't have to live like a monk or train like an Olympian, but you do have to make the only choices that will lead to success. You've got people out there training to beat you. Maybe it's someone at a competing firm. Maybe it's a co-worker who is eyeing the same promotion you are. Correct choices don't help only when competing against other people. You can make choices that lead to behaviors that make you a better spouse. A better parent. A more physically and mentally fit person. You can win even when the opponent is your own previous choices.

A few days after I spoke to the team and coaches about choice, Nick Saban was asked in a press conference about Geno Smith's situation. Nick is famous for using every avenue—including the media—to talk to his players, so even though they'd heard the message from me, he used this question as an opportunity to drive the point even deeper.

"They all think they have this illusion of choice," Saban told the reporters. "Like 'I can do whatever I want to do.' And you kind of have a younger generation now that doesn't always get told no, they don't always get told this is exactly how you need to do it. So they have this illusion that they have all these choices.

"But the fact of the matter is . . . if you want to be good, you really don't have a lot of choices, because it takes what it takes. You have to do what you have to do to be successful. So you have to make choices and decisions to have the discipline and focus to the process of what you need to do to accomplish your goals.

"All these guys that think they have a lot of choices are really sadly mistaken. And I think, as we all have done with our own children, they learn these lessons of life as they get older, and sometimes the best way to learn is from the mistakes that you make, even though we all hate to see them have to make them. And we don't really condone them when they do."

Nick reinforced that message again in July just before preseason camp started. "You know, discipline is a funny thing," he said. "It's not only doing the right thing the right way, the right time all the time. It's making choices and decisions that we all make every day. Discipline to me is here's something that I know I'm supposed to do that I really don't want to do. Can you make yourself do it? And then over here there's something that you know you're not supposed to do that you want to do. Can you keep yourself from doing it? So this is kind of the decision-making that creates a moral compass for all of us to help us do the right things, to stay focused on the process of what we need to accomplish our goals and aspirations, and something that's certainly going to be important for our team to do a good job of if we're going to be able to have the kind of team that we'd like to have."

Once the 2015 season started, the off-field drama ended. But there was plenty of on-field drama. Alabama committed five turnovers in a 43–37 loss at home to Ole Miss, and it felt like the national title dream was dead. But the team had

a lot of good veteran leaders who didn't let their younger
teammates quit on the season just because they'd lost in
the third game. Defensive tackle A'Shawn Robinson was a
bald, bearded 312-pounder who was one of those guys who
always looked older than he was. When he was in high
school in Texas, he was routinely mistaken for a coach. That
year at Alabama, he acted like one. He and fellow defenders
Reggie Ragland, Jonathan Allen, and Dalvin Tomlinson
kept the young guys in line by calling them out in the
locker room every time they didn't make correct choices at
practice or during workouts. Those younger players were
also stud athletes with NFL futures. So why did they listen?
"Do you *see* A'Shawn?" Ragland once asked, cocking his
head toward the guy no one in their right mind would mess
with. (Except Tomlinson, the former high school wrestling
champ who could pin A'Shawn and who had been making
correct choices in the classroom and on the field for years.)
The veterans on that team didn't allow anyone anything
but the correct choices, and that's why that team didn't lose
another game.

That's also why Nick Saban was so proud after Alabama
beat Clemson 45–40 in Glendale, Arizona, to win the
national title. "Every person has two things," Saban said
as workers cleaned confetti off the field. "You can do what
you feel, or you can do what you choose. I told the players,
'I know after fourteen games you guys don't feel like
practicing anymore. I know you probably don't feel all that
great physically. But are you going to choose to do what you

want? Are you going to choose to do the things you need to do to accomplish the goal that you have?' And they did it."

Our challenge every day is to ignore the choice that makes us feel better now so we can make the choice that can help sustain us. Marathon runners tend not to quit on mile twenty-two—even though they would feel much, much better in the moment—because they've stacked up choices that prioritize finishing that freaking race. In many cases, they've adjusted their diets, their sleep schedules, their work schedules. That can't all be for nothing, so they keep running.

The perceived freedom to make any choice without suffering consequences is something a lot of athletes struggle with—particularly on team sports when they leave the structured environment of college for the much less structured life of a professional. If you follow football, you've heard of JaMarcus Russell. He was a supremely talented quarterback at LSU who threw for 3,129 yards and twenty-eight touchdowns in his final season in Baton Rouge. He was six foot six and 265 pounds and could throw a ball eighty yards in the air on a rope. "His passing session was the most impressive of all the pro days I've been to," ESPN draft analyst Todd McShay gushed following Russell's pro day workout at LSU in the spring of 2007. "His footwork for such a big quarterback was surprising. He was nimble in his dropbacks and when he's rolling out and throwing on the run. We all knew coming in that his arm strength is extraordinary. The ball just explodes out of his hands."[2]

Russell had been recruited to LSU by Nick Saban, and
even after Nick left for the Dolphins, Russell was still
under the thumb of then offensive coordinator Jimbo
Fisher. If they want to, college coaches can account for
nearly every waking hour their players are on campus.
They can send graduate assistants to make sure players
are in bed. They can monitor whether or not they went
to class. But that wasn't the case after Russell got picked
number one by the Raiders. He didn't have anyone to hold
his hand, and things went downhill fast after he signed a
six-year contract that included $32 million in guaranteed
money—a deal he didn't agree to until he'd already missed
training camp and the first two weeks of the regular
season.

Russell played in only four games as a rookie. He started
fifteen games in his second season, but he showed up
for training camp his third year weighing 305 pounds.
Less than a year later, the Raiders released him. After
his release, Russell was arrested in Alabama and charged
with possession of codeine syrup without a prescription.
Investigators believed Russell was mixing his own purple
drank, a concoction of codeine, soda, and a flavoring such
as Jolly Rancher candy. The charges were dropped, but the
damage was done. (It didn't help that rapper 2 Chainz went
on ESPN in 2016 and accused Russell of drinking a lot of
lean—purple drank—around that time.) Russell chose not to
take care of his body. He chose not to prepare for games the
way the best quarterbacks in the league did. He chose to

be a bust. "I could have been in better shape," Russell told
ESPN in 2013. "I could have had my weight down. I could
have prepared more, watched more film, whatever. I could
have . . . [done] more."[3]

We can all look back at certain moments in our lives
and say the same thing: I could have done more. I could
have made better choices. The idea is to minimize those
regrets by being honest with yourself about what your
God-given abilities are, choosing to be on a path that jibes
with whatever your life's purpose is, and then making
decisions with that higher goal in mind. Those who can do
that will succeed consistently and those who can't will get
sidetracked and demoralized and will struggle.

Whatever anyone else tells you is noise. Make the choice
to focus on what you are—not on what other people think
you are or should be. Russell Wilson accepts that he's not
six foot three—and yet there was and still is a line of people
waiting to tell him everything he's not. He doesn't focus on
that. A ten-year NFL or NBA veteran lives that way. The
top performer at your company probably also lives this way.
Their real mission and true purpose? Living in alignment
with their visions and being driven to fulfill them. They
are defined by their own behaviors, not by anyone else's
opinion of them. That quality, that ability to determine
one's own true north, is something that unites successful
people across every sport, industry, and military unit I've
ever seen.

We are responsible for telling ourselves what we are. There are options, but not choices. Not really. This is particularly true for those who seek greatness. But remember that everyone has their own formula. Tom Brady has his. Fidelity CEO Abigail Johnson has hers. Alibaba founder Joseph Tsai has his. The Georgia football program has its formula. The members of the special operations community—the Navy SEALs and the army's Rangers and Green Berets, for example— have theirs. As your internal and external worlds change, you've got to *choose* to evolve. The only constant is change, so you have to be willing to examine your choices, to be conscious of your behaviors, and to adapt when you need to.

When you're on a run of correct choices, you need to understand why you made them. Reflect on your successes as much as on your failures. Think about how you got from A to B. Many of the best I've seen had a run on the right side of choices in their lives—whether they knew it or not—and that worked for a time. For some, it worked for a long time. Then they made money. Or they got a significant promotion. And then the pool of options crowded the zone, making the bull's-eye of choice much less clear. Some struggled after finding success because they had made the correct choices early—either out of luck or out of necessity— but didn't fully understand why those choices had brought them success.

Without knowing why you've chosen wisely, you probably won't make correct choices indefinitely. Without the ability to adapt these choices your success will become fleeting. (See former Auburn football coach Gene Chizik, who went from undefeated national champion in the 2010 season to 0–8 in SEC play and was fired after the 2012 season.) This is where neutral thinking can help. Even after great successes, it's wise to step back and take an unbiased look at your circumstances. Then you can formulate a new plan that sets the behaviors (choices) necessary to reach the next goal. If you think you've made it, that you've reached the mountaintop, then you're not going to set any new goals. You're not going to outline behaviors that will allow you to make good choices repeatedly. If you are what you do, then when you don't you aren't. Our choices lead our behaviors, which impact who we become. New behaviors led by new choices create a different you. That different you can be better or worse. Choose better.

We all need guardrails in our lives. For some this is a scale to help us manage our weight. For others it's a quarterly evaluation. For others it's a friend or a partner or a coach who keeps us honest. But what I've learned is that you have to cultivate the ability within yourself to go to the truth. Ask yourself: Do I have what I want right now? If not, could it be that I'm competing against my own choices? If so, fucking stop. Self-esteem is the idea of how you feel about you. We earn these feelings within ourselves both by what we do and by what we don't do. Check in with that daily. You own the six bags of Doritos you ate in the past two weeks. Deal with it. But the seventh bag is in your control right now. No one is mandating an apple or broccoli, so don't act like they are. Win decision one first.

Weight issues resonate with me because of personal history. I was twenty-eight years old and back at Occidental College for an alumni basketball game. At this point I was working at IMG and with US Soccer and had just appeared on ESPN's *Outside the Lines* with soccer player Freddy Adu. It was my first national TV appearance. My career was taking off.

My old basketball coach, Brian Newhall, is one of those "friendly" dicks. He brought me into his office and told me that if I wanted to take the next step as a public figure in the sports world I had to lose twenty-five pounds. My ego rolled onto the floor. "Why the fuck should anyone listen to you at 205?" he asked. I remember that quote sixteen years later like it happened five minutes ago. What was the truth? I had competed at a high level as an athlete into my midtwenties. I had had organizations training me and educating me. I didn't know how to do this for myself. Coach Newhall's comments would lead me down a road that would help me understand the power of liquid calories, sugar, fats, and fast food. But my first choice after that was to not eat food from any place where I could pull up and order it from a box that squawked, "WELCOME TO . . ." My second choice was to exercise more. In the next six months, I lost twenty-one pounds. Since then I have chosen to educate myself about what I put into my body and have chosen to use that knowledge to eat more strategically. I now keep my weight around 165 pounds.

No matter what situation you find yourself in, there is almost always a behavior you can easily identify that, if you eliminate it, will set you on a better path. The first step to getting out of a hole is to stop digging. Sometimes it's easier to *not do* something than it is to *do* something. Stop verbalizing dumb-ass things about your inability to present in front of a group. Stop eating white bread. Stop drinking sugary drinks. Stop watching the news if it makes you mad. Stop saying I can't or I won't or it's impossible. You want something? It starts with one choice.

4

It Takes a Verbal Governor

When I started working with Nick Saban's Alabama football program in 2007, I began building the mental architecture of the team. When Nick took over the program, it still had a great brand name but it had slipped in terms of talent and mindset. Nick was going to recruit better players, and his staff was going to teach them plays and schemes that would work on the football field. I was one of several people Nick used to help train the players' brains.

It wasn't enough to train just the leaders of the team, though. Those guys were already predisposed to do the right things. We needed to reach every player, from the captain on the dean's list to the third-stringer struggling to stay academically eligible, because every one of those players had an effect on our team. For the players to maximize their contributions to the team, we needed them to influence themselves better.

My influence on you has one-tenth the power of your influence on yourself. You have ten times the influence I do when it comes to you. So we understood that with a population of 120 guys, as much as we needed to get our leadership right, we had to get all our players' mindsets right. No one can influence change in their lives like they can. One change would help tremendously, but it would be more difficult to accomplish than you'd think at first. If you've been around a lot of eighteen- to twenty-two-year-olds, maybe you'll appreciate how hard this was.

My goal, my aim, my dream was this: *what if we could get people to just stop saying stupid shit out loud?*

This is what we know. The human mind absorbs negativity seven times more easily than it absorbs positivity. We also know that language is the most powerful carrier of negativity. Thinking about my struggles is nowhere near as powerful as verbalizing them. When it comes out of my mouth, it affects me tenfold. If it's negative it may be seven times more on top of that.

We know negative is more powerful than positive. Study after study has shown people respond more powerfully to negative emotions and experiences than they do to positive emotions and experiences. Ever wonder why people seem to remember all the bad things you said about them and none of the good things? We're hardwired that way. It's an evolutionary trait. In a 2001 article published in the *Review of General Psychology*, the authors examined much of the data on our responses to negative and positive inputs and drew a conclusion that makes a lot of sense.

> From our perspective, it is evolutionarily adaptive for bad to be stronger than good. We believe that throughout our evolutionary history, organisms that were better attuned to bad things would have been more likely to survive threats and, consequently, would have increased probability of passing along their genes. . . . A person who ignores the possibility of a positive outcome may later experience significant regret at having missed an opportunity for pleasure or advancement, but nothing directly terrible is likely to result. In contrast, a person who ignores danger (the possibility of a bad outcome) even once may end up maimed or dead.[1]

But the world has changed. The odds of you walking off an unseen cliff or getting eaten by a bear have dropped considerably. We are relatively safe compared to our long-ago ancestors, so this survival instinct that served them so well serves only to make us miserable much of the time. How miserable? Let's consult the literature.

- A 1990 study published in the *Journal of Clinical Psychology* showed that worriers (negative thinkers) struggled more than non-worriers at completing basic tasks.[2]

- A 2013 study by French researchers and a Georgetown professor found that an "enduring, recurring set of negative judgments, feelings, and behavioral intentions towards another person"—even if it only comes from one or a few people—can have a disproportionately negative effect on an entire population of employees.[3]

- A 2018 study published in *Behaviour Research and Therapy* found that "dampening appraisals"—telling yourself something is too good to last or that you don't deserve it—decreased happiness and increased sadness in study participants.[4]

- A 2015 study in the *Annual Review of Neuroscience* examined multiple previous studies and found that negativity can lead dieters to overeat; can lead people to accept smaller, more immediate rewards instead of bigger, long-term payouts; and can lead to aggressive behavior. Negativity inhibits our ability to delay gratification—even when delaying it would help us in the long run.[5]

- A 2014 study published in *Neurology* linked higher levels of "cynical distrust"—another term for negative thoughts—with a higher incidence of dementia.[6]

In other words, thinking negatively could actually kill you. If that doesn't make you want to learn to think neutrally, I don't know what will. If journal articles are too dry for you, there's some anecdotal evidence from the sports world that should scare the negative right out of you.

Remember Bill Buckner? Even if you don't follow sports, you may have heard of the Boston Red Sox first baseman who let a ground ball hit by the Mets' Mookie Wilson trickle through his legs in the bottom of the tenth inning of game six of the 1986 World Series. Buckner's error allowed Ray Knight to score the game-winning run. The Mets would go on to win game seven and extend a Red Sox title drought that dated back to 1918. Because of that play Buckner— who died in 2019—might be the biggest scapegoat in sports history.

The creepiest part is what Buckner said nineteen days before that game. During an interview with Don Shane of WBZ-TV, Buckner said, "The dreams are that you're gonna have a great series and win. The nightmares are that you're gonna let the winning run score on a ground ball through your legs."[7]

Buckner said it, and it happened. Would Buckner have fielded that ball cleanly had he never said that? We don't know. But the fact that usually sure-gloved Buckner said it out loud means the thought of letting a ball go through his legs was on his mind. Did that thought cross his mind as Mookie Wilson's grounder approached?

Even crazier is a statement basketball star "Pistol" Pete Maravich made to Pennsylvania's *Beaver County Times* reporter Andy Nuzzo in a 1974 interview. "I don't want to play ten years in the NBA and die of a heart attack at age forty," Maravich said.[8] Maravich started his NBA career in 1970. He retired in 1980. That's ten years. Maravich died of a heart attack on January 5, 1988. He was forty. Did his prediction kill him? We don't know. But don't leave it to chance. Stop saying stupid shit out loud.

So how do you shift from negative to neutral? Think of it in dietary terms. The first step to being a better eater is not in being a good one. It's not in dominating broccoli or mastering a plant-based diet. The first step is not being a *bad* eater. Maybe it's eliminating between-meal sweets. Maybe it's swapping potato chips for an apple. Eliminating behaviors is like ordering food from a drive-through. The contemporary philosopher Matthew McConaughey—who also acts a little—says the "process of elimination is the first step" to any serious improvement.[9] One less bad option opens the door for a new and better option to appear more clearly.

We have chances to choose the neutral option nearly every time someone greets us, but how often do we actually select it? We frequently get asked, "How are you?" That has become a substitute for "hello." How do you respond to that question? Do you say

Outstanding

or

Fabulous

or

Okay

or

Shitty?

Or do you just pull a Norm from *Cheers* and say, "It's a dog-eat-dog world and I'm wearing Milk-Bone underwear"[10]?

You choose how you respond to that question. You don't have to say "okay" or "shitty." You don't have to say "outstanding" or "fabulous" either. But the first two responses will affect *you* more negatively than the second two. Negativity affects you negatively 100 percent of the time.

You have to retrain your brain to look at the world differently than it wants to. As I walked out of a Major League clubhouse in 2019, I immediately jumped into a number of meetings scheduled throughout the day with various players, coaches, and executives. I circled back later in the day to one of the team's best players and leaders. I'd had a longtime relationship with him. So he wasn't hearing my message for the first time, even though most of his teammates were. "People truly appreciated the way you spoke," he said. "No bullshit. These are the realities. You were up-front about what eighteen years has taught you, and you got guys thinking less about *having* to be a particular new way and more about being focused on stopping things that are not challenging to stop. You just have to stop."

This was very encouraging. "Did it make sense?" I asked him. "I know it does to you, but I just don't want there to be any debate. Period. No debate. Doesn't mean they have to listen or do any of the shit. Just no debate." He laughed. "Trev, you made that shit real clear." I knew he was referring to the urgency and directness I've learned to speak with in order to survive in the world of sports. Teams give me limited windows at important moments, so I try to be as direct as possible.

The point is simple and it's true. And let me be clear. Bad shit is real. Tough times are real. Many of you reading this book are facing them now, so I don't have to tell you how real they are. Sometimes there isn't much we can do immediately to make our circumstances better. But we can do a number of things to make them worse.

After eighteen years in this field, I've learned that inner voices and those feelings fuck with everyone. But it doesn't have to have the power we think it does. What we say has the power. And those words have an instant link to what we do.

Average is a choice. Greatness is a choice. There is no magic. Only decisions. Great teams behave like great teams.

Their behaviors precede their success. Their behaviors create their belief. Behaviors are not only what we do, but what we are willing to not do.

The choice to verbalize our negativity is a death sentence. Anything you tell yourself inside or—most powerfully— outside about your life is defining your life. That means if shit's not going your way right now, it's not because of a coach or a teammate or a situation. It's you. You have the power to change it. You have the power to prolong it. And the reason you've succeeded and are where you are is not because of things others did or believed *for* you. It's what *you* did and said.

At Alabama, Florida State, and Georgia, we made a bet of sorts. What if we just don't say stupid shit out loud? What if we stopped just that? Period. Alabama has won five national titles since then. FSU has won one. Georgia won an SEC title in Kirby Smart's second season and came a miracle pass away from winning the national title. This stuff works.

The decision to reduce, to eliminate, negativity in your speech is completely within your control. With the negativity reduced, the mind is freed to solve problems more clearly. You'll feel liberated, empowered, accountable for your own life. Stopping negative expression is one of the most powerful steps you can take toward neutral thinking. We acknowledge the past—good or bad—but recognize that what happens next is impacted largely by what we do and say and by what hasn't happened yet.

That group at Alabama had a lot to learn, but those players listened. That first year, the Crimson Tide went 7–6 and lost to Louisiana Monroe—something that should never happen for Alabama. The second year they started off 12–0 but lost the SEC Championship to Florida and the Sugar Bowl to Utah. The third year they went 14–0 and won the national title. They had been paying attention.

Cornerback Javier Arenas was one of the best players on that team. As a high schooler in Tampa, he hadn't received much interest from the big football schools. The Alabama staff before Nick's had taken a flier on him. Before the Tide played Texas for the national title, someone asked Javy if being ignored in recruiting fueled him. He answered,

> I don't think about who didn't recruit me, because that's negative thinking. That's playing mad. I don't think about that. I think about the opportunity and the advantage I've taken so far and how long I'm going to continue to take advantage of it. It's proof that I can do it when there's a shot given, and just take full advantage of it, once again.

That's not positive thinking. That's not unearned confidence. That's a conscious choice to eliminate the negative, combined with a neutral, unbiased assessment of the situation. That's how champions think.

Every time I speak to a new group, the expectation from anyone who knows someone from my field is "same old bullshit about being positive and breathing, etc." I understand the stereotype. I've accepted it. I don't judge it. I have nothing against breathing. But I'm offering something a little different. It's simple—but it's powerful.

If we want to find what that next level is, then the language and the behaviors have to line up with who you want to be, with the outcome you desire. Period. Great teams behave like great teams. Great employees behave like great employees. By the same token, average employees behave like average employees. I respect everyone's right to make that choice. But think more about the things you can stop doing right now—today. Think about putting a muzzle on negative expression for the next twenty-four hours. Negative thoughts can cross your mind. They will. But for one full day forbid yourself from verbalizing them. Witness the difference that makes in your relationships, your mental state, your outcomes. You'll be amazed.

5

It Takes a Negativity Diet

When I was growing up, my dad had basic rules that I believe were created so he could stay at the elite level necessary to do his job. At the time, his job was educating the masses.

My dad wanted me working at an optimum level too. My job was fourth grade.

We both needed to perform. So it made sense that we both should follow the same set of guidelines.

Our rules were simple:

- No national news (local weather and sports were allowed).

- No country music or rhythm and blues.

- The word *can't* was outlawed—in any form.

- No stinkin' thinkin' (no complaining; we are problem solvers, not problem finders).

My dad had a handout that included dozens of classic country song titles. He'd tell his audience that he loved the melodies, but did he really want to consume the negativity?

"If You Don't Believe I Love You, Just Ask My Wife"

"Sleeping Single in a Double Bed"

"Thank God and Greyhound"

"You Blacked My Blue Eyes Once Too Often"

"Does My Ring Hurt Your Finger"

"She Got the Gold Mine (I Got the Shaft)"

"You're the Reason Our Kids Are Ugly"

As a child, I just accepted these rules as reality. I had no deep longing to listen to country music. I didn't know any different. But looking back on these rules as an adult, I see now that my dad wasn't trying to mandate the way we thought but rather trying to slow the flow of the forces of negativity from the outside world and stem their effects. So much of what we do is dictated by our state of mind, the way we feel. Much of the world seems out of our control, but the fact is you have the power to decide what influences come into your home. The news directly targets our negative-leaning tendencies. Programming on Bravo and many other channels weaponizes husbands against wives, wives against husbands. Music can lift us up or tear us down. We all know this.

But where do we screw this up? We screw it up by not choosing to control the pieces of our lives that are in our control. The clicker is in your hands. You turn that car radio on or off. You decide which app to download. You choose which websites to visit and who to save or delete on your phone. Your excuses?

- My boss is an asshole.

- My co-workers are dickheads.

- The people around me don't support or believe in me.

I get it. I believe you. And you just described a day in the life of many of the best athletes as they get ready to do their jobs in front of 80,000 people. But this is the point: does a bad 50 percent of your day give you the right to concede the other 50 percent? I don't think so—not if you live within a neutral mindset. That makes *you* responsible for the next moment. You are not required to live in the past. A job can be a brutal environment. Many are, but that doesn't mean your home has to be.

When you finish this book there will be no debate that
negative thinking, language, content consumption, and
people will fuck you up. And no one influences how you
navigate all of that like *you* do. Period. Think of it in
nutritional terms. Before I can tell you how to eat well,
I have to get you to stop eating like shit. After a whole
pizza, an apple won't help. So let's start by stopping after
a few slices. After a day of slaying yourself with your
external talk followed by four hours of the wrong TV and
music, I can promise you that the meditation app you just
downloaded is not going to help. Neither will the five bullet-
point mantras on your fridge.

If you need further proof, I am your guinea pig.

In late 2018, I was talking to a friend who had just retired
from twenty-five years in the navy, the last fifteen as
a SEAL. He was a breacher. These are the baddest of
bad dudes. They're the first guys in, and they've seen
adversity most of us can't even imagine. Like many in that
community, my friend is pretty private. He'd prefer I didn't
reveal his name, but I can tell you what he did for me.

As we talked, I was open with my friend about the ass-
beating of challenges I was facing in 2018 as I navigated the
world as an unexpectedly single person with a business that
was gaining traction. I had to relearn how to meet people.
I had to manage success and adversity simultaneously
and ride through them. He responded with a classic SEAL

way of looking at adversity: in the middle of a period of adversity, we have an opportunity to stress-test our own belief system.

"What do you mean?" I asked.

He said that if I truly believed that negativity was the real competitor, then I should live in it while I'm in these tough moments of my life. He wanted me to see if my behaviors could outcompete negativity, if my language could outcompete it. He told me to bring constant negativity into my life like most people do on a daily basis. He encouraged me to live one of the lessons I teach.

My first thought: What the fuck? The real goal, I thought, should be to utilize what I'd learned to navigate through this time. I've spent almost half my life teaching people how to develop good behaviors. Now he was asking me to engage in bad behaviors—on purpose? But his point was that I needed to test what I taught to ensure first that it's correct and second that I'm teaching it correctly. This made sense. It might make it easier to teach some of these lessons if I actually lived them. I was in. And so began a monthlong challenge that would cement many of the views that permeate this book.

An attitude is a habit of thinking. It is formed in the same way we learn to be good or bad at anything—through repetition (or lack of it). We weren't born with attitudes.

They get shaped from a young age. In the beginning, I'm not who I think I am. I'm actually who you think I am. A four-year-old may smile up to 500 times a day. An adult? Fifteen times. As a teacher who worked in both middle school and high school, it was incredible for me to see attitudes and mentalities evolve or devolve as students grew older.

Converse ran an ad in the 1970s that said, "Champions are not born. They're made." What if the inverse is what's really true—that a champion might actually be born, then unmade? The entire year of 2018 had felt the way I imagine climbing Mount Everest might feel. So I thought, "Fuck it. I can't make it any worse. I can only learn." I took on the challenge to expose myself to more negativity than I ever had before. My family's rules had kept me away from much of the negativity that most people bombard themselves with on a daily basis. Those rules—which I had carried into adulthood—made me different, but they also made me an excellent subject for this experiment. I would introduce a flood of external negativity. We would learn what effect, if any, it had on my mind and my daily life. This was the plan:

- Live each day and execute each task normally.

- Add three to four hours of external stimuli to drive negative noise into my mind via my phone and car stereo.

- These external stimuli to induce negativity would include

—an hour of news from my least favorite news station. Regardless of your political affiliation or channel of choice, the business model of today's 24-hour news channels is to make you mad, scared, or—preferably— both. They want you to think the world will end if the person you don't like wins an election. They want you to think there are kidnappers waiting around every corner to steal your children. This keeps you watching. It also bombards you with negative thoughts and helps you generate your own.

—an hour to an hour and a half of hard-core metal rock. There's a reason they blast this stuff to break hostages in movies and in real life.

—an hour to an hour and a half of new country music. Remember the old joke about country music? If you listen to it backward, you get your wife, your truck, *and* your dog back? Unfortunately, I would listen to it as intended. That would mean a lot of lost wives, trucks, and dogs.

- I would listen to the music in the morning during any exercise I did and in the afternoon and evening while traveling. At home or in hotels I would consume whatever I normally would, but would see if I began to choose different programming.

- Monitor the impact by letting the people I work most closely with know what I'd done and seek their feedback. Internally I would monitor my text messages

over the course of thirty days to see how my tone and
the people I contacted would change.

What did I hope to gain?

This was my version of *Super Size Me*, the documentary
that has Morgan Spurlock eating only McDonald's for a
month. He went in with the idea that the effects would be
deleterious; he had no idea that they would be catastrophic.
I wouldn't be experimenting with fast food. I had chosen an
equally competitive enemy—stupid shit going into my brain.
This wouldn't harden my arteries like cholesterol would. It
would harden my attitudes and obscure my vision.

Over the course of that month, my resolve steadily
weakened. Of all the content that impacted me, it was the
country music that gut-punched the shit out of me daily.
I must have listened to Sam Hunt's "Cop Car" more than
800 times. I downloaded every version of it on YouTube
Premium.

Over the monthlong experiment, the constant barrage of
negativity made me burrow into the real weaknesses in
my life and created the most unfamiliar of feelings in me:
doubt. Would I ever meet someone again? If I did, would
she have any interest in me? If I suck ass now, then maybe I
should look back in the past and see if there's someone who
would remember me from before I got my ass booted? Can
this new business work?

Anything new or unknown began to feel like a guaranteed failure. I became someone who feared driving on the freeway. I felt comfortable only on the simplest of roads in old, familiar neighborhoods.

I met with NBA teams, spent time around the biggest college football games, and continued to speak to and work with many of the top companies. But inside, I was crumbling. I was severely fucked up. If there was any upside, it was that my empathy for people in adversity and facing challenges increased. I took inventory of that, but I understood the idea of psychogenic death a lot better.

What is that? Dr. John Leach, a research fellow at the University of Portsmouth in England, coined the term "give-up-itis" to describe how people can lose their will to live and actually die following extreme trauma. Leach studied stories of people in Korean prisoner-of-war camps and in concentration camps and published an article in the journal *Medical Hypotheses* that attempted to map the stages of psychogenic death. The first, Leach writes, is social withdrawal. The person stops interacting with those around him. The second stage is apathy, where the person can't find the energy to keep going. Leach calls the third stage aboulia. It combines a lack of motivation with a dampened emotional response and an inability to make decisions. The fourth stage, which Leach calls psychic akinesia, is an even steeper drop in motivation. This stage can be marked by a lack of response to physical pain. The fifth stage, according to Leach, is death. The person may still have access to enough clean air, food, and water to live, but their mind has essentially given up on life. They have, for lack of a better term, lost the will to live. And that is followed by actual death.

I wasn't anywhere near that point, but I was heading in that direction as my experiment continued. The text messages from the final week are crazy. They scare me the most because they're in a language that I don't speak. I sent one of baseball's great players and a longtime friend a text that said, "This uncertainty is terrifying." He knew that didn't sound like me. It wasn't true either. He responded, "Trev, if you focus on the feelings you are focusing on they will drown you."

I was texting preachers daily. Guys I didn't know. A guy in North Carolina—lovely man—but I hadn't even heard of him before I found him online while seeking out ways to climb out of the hole I found myself in.

One note I sent to Russell Wilson's pastor, Judah Smith, sums up where I was headed: "You tell me any day in LA, bro. I could really use your perspective. I will come to you."

By the end I was consuming media in my house that I never had before. I watched movies like *When a Man Loves a Woman*. Watching *Meg Ryan?* That was not me.

I consumed cable news and embarked on behavior patterns that didn't resemble anything I'd done before. When I went to bed. Where I fell asleep. Where I'd go to hike. Where I'd go to eat. What time I'd go to the office. How I'd talk to others.

After an event in Chicago with Russell's brother, Harrison, and our other business partner, DJ Edison, I was on a plane back to Phoenix when the psychological symptoms began to feel physical. I felt sadness and fatigue, like an oil from an *X-Files* episode slowly permeating me. I had the row to myself, and the plane was dark. Tears began flowing. I put my hands on my cheeks to stop the tears, and suddenly I felt overwhelmed and scared.

I jumped up and went to the bathroom and washed my face. Back in my seat, I put on one of Russell's highlight videos that we had just made. I put on some Hillsong UNITED, hoping the harmonies would lift me up the way they lift Russell. But it could only mask the symptoms.

I got home and went to bed, but awoke at 1:38 a.m. in tears. The house was pitch-black. I was by myself. I walked down the stairs, then went out to get the mail. And I knew that I was done. The experiment was over. After twenty-six days, I had broken. The past behind me was clear. The future was fog. On October 31st, 2018, at 4:32 p.m., I sent an email to Russell, Harrison, and DJ to explain what had been going on with me the previous weeks.

Russ/HW/DJ,

In a discussion with a close peer of mine in the special operations community, I made a choice to test the concept of neutral thinking and the power of language in my own personal "resilience training." We tested the goal of implementing proper use of neutral language versus the steady power of negative mood influencers implemented through the medium of music. We agreed that I would be the test subject.

Negative music and sounds are a big part of the hostage process relative to torture . . . and believe me I know this all sounds crazy . . . But in concert with isolation and physiological torture, negative stimuli—like music—has created a phenomenon (as demonstrated in the Korean War) called "give-up-itis."

The hypothesis was that my strong level of adversity tolerance would not be able to last twenty-eight days under the influx of three hours of country music daily. I charted my music, text messages, language, TV watching, etc., and listened on Pandora and YouTube to

    Jake Owen
    Sam Hunt
    Keith Urban

I was able to chart my music via the "thumbs up" feature on Pandora and wrote my choices down daily.

I listened to this music on every flight, every hike, every walk to the mailbox, every pregame bus ride. In the car I listened only to news radio.

CONCLUSIONS

The Outcomes Were Clear

While there were a handful of positive outcomes—namely more empathy and a deeper emotional connection to some clients—the vast majority of the impact was pretty brutal, and I've got most of it tabulated.

- My sense of internal pessimism and personal doubt about my future exploded. No matter the steady diet of neutral statements or attempts to control my language and what I consumed on the internet, I felt a huge sense of terror that is very clear in my text messages beginning October 20th.

- I reverted to things and people from the past. I tried to find stability there as I could see only fog socially, health-wise, personally, and business-wise going forward.

- I cancelled two doctor's appointments—including my dentist—in this window, believing they would give me terrible news and I couldn't deal with it.

- I could fall asleep, but would wake up after a few hours with levels of anxiety that were completely foreign to me and pace the house. I usually don't feel anxiety ever, about anything.

- During the last week there were periods, mostly at night, when I felt as if I were walking on broken ice, and I had hyperemotional periods during the day.

- I awoke at 1:38 a.m. one night and couldn't stop crying. It was only the second or third time I've cried since 1999, when my dad was diagnosed with multiple myeloma. I had no idea where the tears were coming from.

I called the friend who suggested this experiment to me and acknowledged that I had been broken in twenty-six and a half days.

So why the f would I do this?

The year 2018 was one of the most toxic in the history of our country. There was negativity everywhere. In our news. Our music. Our podcasts. I believed I could beat external influencers with my own internal language. I was wrong. I don't think our own language can work nearly as well if we continue to consume emotional mediums—like music or brutal news—that weaponize negativity. They rendered forty-plus years of psychological strategies ineffective because I was in a place of brutal despair.

Below is another email I sent to Russell, Harrison, and DJ:

THE KEY LEARNING

My father always said that HOPE was the most powerful weapon of all. If we don't become hopeless, then we won't become helpless. The constant barrage of sad melodies and music made even me feel broken and scared. Hugely foreign concepts to my world and my well-protected (and engineered) brain. Simply put—MAKE HOPE A HABIT.

At present, I am on a two-day detox from any music and any news and any radio. Since I don't get to compete on a field like RW anymore, I accepted this challenge to strengthen our teaching by emphasizing in TANDEM both language and the external, controllable consumption of external content (news/music).

Thank YOU all!
Trev

Russell's brother responded:

Trev,

Thanks for sharing this, man. We got your back! And we also look up to you.

This IS AUTHENTICITY.

Love ya, man
Harry

So what did I learn? Negativity, in any form that we choose to bring into our lives, is poison. There is negativity outside of our lives that we can't stop and can't stay away from. But we can choose what we bring into our lives. Don't choose the things that will weaponize us against ourselves. Stay away from cable news channels. Stay away from radio shows and podcasts designed to inflame and anger. Nothing personal against Sam Hunt, but stay away from sad country songs. Life is hard enough even when we don't choose to bombard our senses with negativity. When we do, everything can feel hopeless. So watch shows that make you laugh or cheer. Consume news that deals in facts, not opinions. Listen to songs that lift you up instead of dragging you down.

I'm a warrior. I believe my adversity tolerance is as elite as you'll ever see. I folded in twenty-six days. It's not a fair fight. So choose not to fight it. Choose not to assault your senses with negativity.

You'll be happier. You'll also find it easier to stay neutral. And that will help you master the next skill you'll learn—creating an ad campaign in your brain.

6

It Takes an Ad Campaign
in Your Brain

Marketing is one of the most powerful resources businesses have at their disposal. Advertising works. Marketing moves products. More specifically, great marketers move people, and *that* moves products (even when people don't need the products). A world-class sports team can create buy-in and belief only by marketing a powerful vision to the players, coaches, and staffers it employs. The ability to sell to others is incredibly valuable, but it isn't as valuable as the ability to sell to yourself.

When I was young my dad would tell me, "No one will ever influence Trevor Moawad the way Trevor will influence himself." He was right. The marketing he was talking about is the gateway to success in our inner world.

Without this skill set, I believe the personal challenges I faced in 2018 may have led me to clinical depression. They didn't. I understand this now because I know exactly how to internally market to myself. I've lived it. I've seen it. I've watched it, and the best "choose" to do it. This type of advertising is one of the most important fundamentals every individual must master if they want to be successful.

When I stood in front of the Florida State football team for the first time after getting hired by Jimbo Fisher, I opened by asking the team—coaches and players—one question:

How many of you over the course of a day find yourself talking to yourself through an internal voice?

About a quarter of the players raised a hand. I then addressed the 75 percent who didn't raise a hand. "Those who didn't hold that hand up are probably asking themselves, 'I don't know. *Do* I talk to myself?'" That got a big laugh, but it also taught those guys an important lesson. We all talk to ourselves, whether we say the words out loud or keep them inside our minds. We have an inner conversation that runs constantly. Some of us may occasionally have a conversation out loud with ourselves, but 100 percent of us talk to ourselves internally. Go ahead and try it. Tell yourself, "I'm not going to talk to myself anymore." What did you say back? "No way"? "Sure"? Either way, you just talked to yourself after trying to stop talking to yourself. We all have conversations with ourselves. It's okay if you choose not to believe that. You'd just be wrong. It's like gravity. Gravity is real. You don't see it, but it still affects you.

So now that we've established that we all talk to ourselves, it's time to understand that everything we say matters. Obviously the words we say out loud to other people matter, but the words we say in our own heads are just as important. Because we have more power over ourselves than anyone else does.

Words are tools, and they both predict and perpetuate performance. At a young age I learned that there are two types of influence and marketing: marketing from the outside in (commercials, billboards, what other people tell us) and marketing from the inside out (our own internal monologue). Where does the real power come from? The external or the internal? The truth is that it comes from both. But the scope of the influence on us isn't equal. That internal conversation influences all of us more.

If you accept the basic science of influence on any level, there is an element of genetics and an element of conditioning. We call it nature vs. nurture. In *Hard Optimism: How to Succeed in a World Where Positive Wins*, Price Pritchett writes that 25 percent of who we become is predetermined by the genes we inherited from our parents.[1] The rest comes from how we are conditioned externally. Our environment. Our culture. Our socioeconomic reality. Our family.

The world has chosen to view this 75 percent as largely external environments, external cultures, or external realities—usually out of our control. To hear most people tell it, the equations look like this: fucked-up environment = fucked-up people; great environment = great people. My dad didn't see it that way—not in what he taught, not in what he lived, and not for his son. My dad lived in a world grounded in truth, and bad shit happens. My dad partnered that with another reality, however: we all create our own internal environment. Our own internal culture. Our socioeconomic status or family life or time with friends are realities, but we control how we interpret them.

My dad's influence on me? One-to-ten. Mine on myself? Ten-to-one. So my words—not his words—would matter most. No one will be able to influence me like I will be able to influence me. This is particularly true when the words come out of my mouth and start immediately connecting to behaviors. Words become self-fulfilling prophecies. So if I created an internal ad campaign that presents me as a loser no one would want to listen to, I would act as if my talents didn't matter. I'd wonder why anyone would want to read this book. And that would make it very difficult to write this book. Instead, my internal ad campaign during this process is a series of neutral statements that explain exactly why I'm writing this book:

- Some of the best players and coaches in sports have hired me to help train their brains.

- That training has resulted in improved performance, and clients have told me both verbally and with their actions (by continuing to hire me) that they believe the training to be effective.

- While a small part of what I teach applies only to elite athletes and coaches, most of what I teach is applicable to people in any walk of life. This could help everyone. So I want to reach the largest possible audience.

Advertising works on all of us. Remember this tune? "Two all-beef patties, special sauce, lettuce, cheese, pickles, onions—on a sesame-seed bun!"

I don't want to remember that, yet I do, because Ray Kroc and McDonald's did an incredible job. Sometimes when I'm driving at night, those Golden Arches feel like the Death Star and I'm Han Solo in the Millennium Falcon. I respect the fries, but for me, the Big Mac attack usually happens after I eat the burger. So yes, advertising works. That's why it's a multibillion-dollar industry.

When I speak to groups, I remind them that in 1988 Nike was trying to catch Reebok. It's tough to believe now that Nike is the biggest athletic apparel company in the world, but there was a time it wasn't so dominant. According to the *New York Times*, in 1988 Nike had $1.2 billion in sales compared to Reebok's $1.79 billion. So what happened? Yes, Michael Jordan led the NBA in scoring with thirty-five points a game and won MVP in 1988, so that helped sales of his signature shoe. But that was only one piece of Nike's attempt to reposition itself in the shoe and apparel market. The biggest piece of that repositioning was an ad campaign built around something a convicted murderer had said just before he was executed by firing squad.

In 1977, a man from Oregon named Gary Gilmore was executed in Utah. Before the firing squad fired, Gilmore was asked if he had any final thoughts. "Let's do it," he said.

Dan Wieden, one of the founders of the Wieden+Kennedy ad agency, lived in Portland and had followed the case. In 1988, he was trying to come up with a tagline for a new series of Nike commercials. He remembered what Gilmore had said. "I didn't like 'Let's do it,'" Wieden told *Dezeen* in 2015. "So I just changed it to 'Just do it.'"[2]

The groups I speak to, whether they're athletes, soldiers, or office workers, can repeat those three words with almost no prompting:

Just do it.

That's how influential that slogan was, even though Wieden claims Nike founder Phil Knight rejected the slogan at first. "Phil Knight said, 'We don't need that shit,'" Wieden told *Dezeen*. "I said, 'Just trust me on this one.' So they trusted me and it went big pretty quickly."[3]

Big? It went huge. That may be the most memorable advertising slogan of my lifetime, and I have a theory why. It's neutral. It doesn't promise anything good will happen once you "do it." It doesn't promise anything bad will happen if you don't do it. It just commands you to do *it*, whatever *it* is. You dream up the rest. That's incredibly powerful.

You may not get paid like Dan Wieden does, but you produce multiple ad campaigns every day. That dialogue going on inside your mind creates the ads. It creates your brand.

No one knows exactly how many thoughts you have a day. The estimates range anywhere from 60,000 to 120,000. Whatever it actually is, it's a lot. Your brain is constantly evaluating situations. The key is to learn to control those thoughts in order to advertise to yourself. Because you are the most powerful advertiser.

My dad liked to say that the human mind is the fastest, coolest, most compact and efficient computer ever produced in large quantities by unskilled labor. He once said this to 10,000 people at a Starbucks event in Orlando with CEO Howard Schultz in 2005. I was with my dad at that event. I stayed up with him at the hotel at Disney World that entire night. He was preparing to attempt his third bone marrow transplant—which meant his body was about to get its ass beat—and he had just finished a round of chemo. But his educational system, Increasing Human Effectiveness, had

been disseminated to Starbucks' 18,000 employees, and
he was scheduled to keynote their national event. As he
leaned over the toilet and gasped for air—all fucking night—
there was no doubt he felt this was an inconvenience to
him and it was real, but what I saw was that he believed
he could "behave himself" through it. I was about thirty.
I was already leading the mental conditioning element
for the Jacksonville Jaguars and US Soccer and was the
director of mental conditioning at IMG Academy. I'd been
promoted after my partner, Chad, had left to be the New
York Yankees' director of optimal performance. I had seen,
learned, experienced, and participated in some incredible
feats where greatness was required. I had seen incredible
performances by Fred Taylor, Freddy Adu, Alex Smith,
Clint Mathis, Eli Manning, Tony Romo, Anquan Boldin,
and Byron Leftwich, and by players in youth World Cups
and in the US Open and more. But what I saw that night
showed me the mind's incredible power in a way that other
feats hadn't. This was a different type of greatness. This
greatness fueled survival. It came from the same place. The
mind is incredible.

The will to succeed in life or in the fight of your life is
rooted deep within your own beliefs. It is how we sell
ourselves on what has happened, what could happen, and
what will happen to us. Within this internal ad campaign
that we create for ourselves, a neutral approach, based on
attainable behaviors, moves us steadily in alignment with
that vision.

The law of substitution tells us we can keep only one thought in our minds at a time. Those thoughts may change from moment to moment, but we function best when we're broadcasting a series of strong, neutral statements to ourselves and don't let outside noise or our own internal chatter derail those thoughts. The best athletes—the best performers in any field—are masters at making sure they keep their internal ad campaign neutral and consistent with the task at hand.

Let's take a little test to see how good you are at focusing your personal ad campaign. The first part you can do by yourself, but you'll need a friend or a family member to help you with the next two parts.

For the first part, you're going to have sixty seconds. So grab your smartphone and set the timer for a minute. On the next page you'll see a grid with the numbers 0 through 99, arranged randomly. (Don't flip the page and peek—you'll only cheat yourself.) When you get to the end of this page, I'll give you a number. When you flip the page, your job will be to find that number and cross it out with an X. Then you'll find the next number in consecutive descending order. You'll repeat this until your buzzer sounds. Then you'll count how many numbers you crossed out.

Your number is . . . 83. GO!

84	27	51	78	59	52	13	85	61	55
28	60	92	04	97	90	31	57	29	33
32	96	65	39	80	77	49	86	18	70
76	87	71	95	98	81	01	46	88	00
48	82	89	47	35	17	10	42	62	34
44	67	93	11	07	43	72	94	69	56
53	79	05	22	54	74	58	14	91	02
06	68	99	75	26	15	41	66	20	40
50	09	64	08	38	30	36	45	83	24
03	73	21	23	16	37	25	19	12	63

Score: _____

That was a little tougher than you thought it would be, wasn't it? Well, get ready, because most people find this next one tougher. Find a family member, a friend, a co-worker, or a kind stranger. Reset your timer to a minute. You'll be doing the same thing, but the person helping you will be staring at you silently the entire time.

Are you ready?

Your number is . . . 77. GO!

66	34	82	28	73	56	42	63	07	72
85	94	01	15	83	90	11	38	92	43
10	75	62	21	08	35	67	52	16	30
29	81	47	98	44	88	26	57	55	23
97	39	71	24	50	78	74	02	96	80
51	68	03	64	17	93	22	84	09	59
18	27	46	54	31	12	40	14	48	36
91	86	13	00	05	37	60	69	32	76
49	06	33	58	77	65	45	19	99	61
25	89	41	95	20	70	87	53	04	79

Score: _____

How did you do? Was that easier or harder? Most people find it harder. The person watching us isn't saying anything, but being observed tends to make us more self-conscious. That can disrupt or change the dialogue we're having with ourselves. What did you think as you searched for each number? Did you worry that the person watching thought you were stupid if you couldn't find them fast enough? Did you worry about what they thought of you at any point? I bet that if you did, it made finding those next numbers harder. That's because those thoughts replaced the thoughts you needed to be thinking to find the next number. After you found 77, your only thought should have been "find 76." Most people aren't wired that way. But you can rewire yourself.

Don't let that friend wander off to make a sandwich. You're going to need their help one more time. And they're probably going to enjoy this one. Reset your timer to a minute. Now tell your friend that when you start, they need to trash talk you mercilessly. Okay, maybe not completely mercilessly—no touching, no four-letter words. But within those rules, tell them to say whatever they think they need to say to distract you.

Are you ready?

Are they ready?

Your number is . . . 33. GO!

19	00	95	60	25	83	97	93	52	24
40	06	77	69	15	98	08	78	61	54
84	14	26	62	48	36	22	34	04	47
88	82	55	87	01	41	39	18	58	89
21	68	09	33	44	53	43	73	64	13
28	74	57	80	65	70	10	27	81	91
46	38	16	23	49	17	30	76	05	51
03	75	42	63	02	59	90	20	32	67
29	66	11	71	45	94	12	37	56	85
35	92	31	50	86	99	79	96	07	72

Score: _____

Okay. Count them up. How many did you get? For most people, that last round has the lowest score. And while it seems like an external factor—the trash talk—caused you to struggle, it really was your own inner dialogue. If your mind had kept saying "find 32," it would have found 32 faster. But once it said, "Wait, how did she know *that?*" it stopped saying "find 32." You can train yourself to keep running the "find 32" commercial instead of letting your brain change the channel. But it takes practice. As you go about daily tasks, pay attention to how often your mind drifts. Bring it back to the task at hand by telling yourself exactly what you need to do. Think back to Russell and his keys to the 2014 season:

- Great fundamentals

- Great balance

- Be engaged

When chaos swirled around him, Russell centered himself by focusing on one of those three things. They brought him back to neutral and allowed him to keep executing. That internal ad campaign pushed out all other thoughts and allowed him to focus only on what mattered.

So Here You Are

In early 2006, cameras and producers filled the rooms in our team center at IMG Academy as I prepared to brief ten high-value football prospects on the path that lay ahead of them. I stood up front with super agent Tom Condon and Fox Sports host Rob Stone. Behind us were a team of IMG's top marketers and world-class physical and nutritional performance coaches. This year would be chronicled by producer Don Argott for a documentary called *Two Days in April*. Once finished, the film would hit the festival circuit and be purchased by Starz. It would go on to become one of Netflix's most powerful sports documentaries. The film focuses on four NFL draft prospects as they journey from dormant success to utilized potential. My role would be to make sure those four gave themselves the best chance to succeed.

"So here you are," I said. "Thousands of miles from Oklahoma. Thousands more from Boston College. A country away from Arizona State. All of you have chosen to be here and all of you were chosen to be here. This academy? It is known as the world's toughest playground, and it is your home for the next three months. This is where the best come to get better."

I had just been through this process with Eli Manning and Alex Smith and I'd seen them go number one in the draft. Alex would slightly "out-behavior" California's Aaron Rodgers, and the difference was nearly $20 million on the first contract. (Aaron has done quite well for himself since.) Their decisions and their ability to exert their own influence on themselves over the next few months could have lifelong financial ramifications. How they behaved between that point and the NFL draft could make them millions or cost them millions.

"Your past is over," I said. "Your future is uncertain, and the unknown is uncomfortable. I understand it. Every prospect that has sat here faced similar challenges. The brochure hits on a lot that have succeeded, but they haven't all carried that weight. That's the truth. Having said that, the path is clear. The recipe is defined. You are here because of what we've helped others do. We have earned the right to be here, because we've helped others dominate and that pays our salaries. But let me be clear. You will run. Not us. You will do the interviews. Not us. You will have the twenty-hour days. Not us. And you will be the one looking in the mirror when this process ends. You. Not us."

From a young age, I've embraced the chance to lead. The "how" never changes. The "who" certainly has. The consequences were significant here and, like my father wanting to make sure my voice had the real power, the players needed to understand that their own influence would ultimately decide their outcomes.

"Let me ask you guys something," I said. "You ever have— over the course of a day—a voice inside your mind that talks to you? Not out loud. But inside." Half of the hands went up. "I see Mathias [Kiwanuka] has his hand up. Derek [Hagan] as well. Clint [Ingram] is sitting in the back—hands down—asking himself right now . . . 'I don't think I talk to myself' . . . while he talks to himself."

Everyone in the room burst out laughing. Clint's teammate Travis Wilson started grabbing him. "The reality is we all talk to ourselves," I said. "And even if you say, 'Fuck this dude Trevor. I'm not talking to myself anymore,' you'd be thinking that while you were continuing to do what you just said you wouldn't do."

The room laughed again.

"This is the truth," I said. "There are going to be psychological realities that you won't see the same way the physical ones appear, but they will have similar influence on this process for you. If you leave here ignorant, then that's our fault. So every element of your athleticism will be trained—including your mentality. Why? Because the NFL requires intentionality. There are no accidents."

Years later, that point would be reinforced for me by a client who reached the pinnacle of the league. I asked Russell Wilson what he told himself when he played in his first Super Bowl against the Broncos in February 2014. "It's focusing on a few simple basics," he said. "Footwork, balance, checklist. You're not worrying about the play before—how good it was, how bad it was. Focus on this play. What is the mission on this play? You're trying to focus on one thing at a time." (As you've probably guessed, this list evolved into the checklist you saw a few pages ago that helped guide Russell the entire next season.)

Notice that Russell didn't talk about the Broncos' defense or the Patriots' defense. Yes, he was aware that there were 300-pound dudes trying to rip his head off, but he had prepared for them. His teammates had prepared for them. His coaches had prepared for them. The only way they could throw him off his game was by cancelling the commercial in his head and forcing his thoughts elsewhere. Instead, Russell kept repeating the same neutral thoughts to keep himself focused even though the entire world was watching. Think about that. His influence outweighed the world's influence.

Russell pointed out that this method of internal dialogue works outside the Super Bowl as well. "A lot of it is because of the distractions our world presents to us. We lose track of the moment," he said. "We lose track of how important being in the moment is. You have to be able to focus on the moment. In our relationships, in our friendships, in our sport, in our field, just be in the moment as much as you can."

"Clarity is key," he said. "I know my mission. I know what I need to accomplish. Let's go do it."

What you hear clearly from Russell is marketing. It's an ad campaign. It's scripted. It's clear. It steers his behavior. It focuses his choices. And yes, it is neutral. It is, in fact, Russell Wilson's commercial. One he has created and refined on his path to his own success.

This marketing is available to all of us. You are doing it right now as you read this. Start simply with this mission:

What three behaviors will help get me to where I want to be?

Write those three behaviors in first person, present tense form. If going to the gym will get you what you want, write "I go to the gym."

"Just do it" is a call to action. It's time you make a similar call to yourself.

7

It Takes Visualizing

Growing up, my favorite nights were the ones when my dad was home from one of his frequent work trips and had time to tuck me into bed. Music was a big part of the educational programs my father created, and he'd communicate powerful messages in entertaining songs. It was part of his genius. He'd usually come into my room with his ukulele and we'd sing a song he called "Stinkin' Thinkin'."

> *"We don't care what the other schools do.*
> *We don't allow no stinkin' thinkin' at our school."*

I'd wind up using the core concepts of that song in my own teaching, only instead of telling elementary school students to eliminate stinkin' thinkin', I'd tell college football players to stop saying stupid shit out loud. I loved that song, and I loved those nights. But one night when I was eight years old, my dad didn't bring his ukulele into the room. Instead, he sat down and asked me, "Do you understand the power of a dream?"

"Yes," I replied. "You can do anything you want in a dream, Dad, because they're not real."

"But what if they *were* real?" he said. "Tonight, I want you to really understand the power of your dreams."

He asked me to imagine sitting at the dinner table, ready for Mom to bring in my favorite casserole. He asked me to remember the smells. The room. The lighting. I could see all of it so clearly, even though I was on a different floor of the house.

"As the casserole comes, imagine that you are very hungry," he said. "You just got back from soccer practice. But Mom says that before you can eat it she needs you to bite into this lemon first."

"A lemon, Dad?" I asked.

"Yes," he said. "If you want dinner."

He asked me to pretend the lemon was in my hand. To look at it. To examine its yellow skin. He repeated that the only thing between me and the casserole was the lemon. He told me to put the lemon in my right hand and to bring it toward me slowly and then to take a giant bite. He told me to feel the juice coming down my face.

I immediately winced. *"DAD!"* I screamed.

"Could you taste it?" he replied.

"Yes," I said. "It was awful!"

"But I thought you said dreams weren't real, son," he said. "If they weren't, then how could you taste the lemon?"

He told me this was what he called "possibility thinking." He told me that nothing is impossible if we can see it first in our minds.

It's thirty-five years later, and I still don't exactly understand what it was I was tasting that night. Our minds struggle to distinguish between what is real and what is imagined. We've all been there. Remember that class in high school when you dozed off and then jerked awake because you were sure you were falling? Maybe you stayed awake through all your classes, but I guarantee you've had moments when you were certain something was real only to learn later that it was all in your mind. The 1999 film *The Matrix* was built upon these psychological principles that we unconsciously experience daily.

"What is real?" the character Morpheus asks hero Neo. "How do you define real? If you're talking about what you can feel, what you can smell, what you can taste and see, then real is simply electrical signals interpreted by your brain."[1]

I shared this clip in our second team meeting with the Jacksonville Jaguars as they prepared to play the Philadelphia Eagles. Coach Tom Coughlin modified the practice schedule to make time for us to drive a powerful point home to the players. Though the media and pundits had given this nationally televised game to the Eagles already, we explained that our reality would be different. Real is ultimately what we do and what we do is influenced by how we see reality. Our goal was to remind the team of "possibility thinking." This is the idea of believing in an outcome in advance of evidence because you have visualized that outcome.

Imagery is a mental technique. It's a core element of any mental conditioning program—just as squats are a core element of any physical conditioning program. Structured imagery programs the mind and the body to respond optimally by recreating or creating information using all the senses—sight, touch, hearing, taste, smell. It's exactly what my father had me do at age eight. Your brain strengthens your muscle memory by teaching the fibers in your muscles how to move as if you were actually performing what you imagine. So when you see that lemon entering your mouth, your taste buds respond and learn as if they were actually tasting. This is real. We all do this. We all can do it better. The best do it strategically.

In 1996, Michael Johnson ground his gold shoes into the starting blocks, and 82,884 people in Atlanta's Olympic stadium fell silent. Johnson already had won the 400-meter gold medal. He had blown away the field, in fact. This race, the 200 meters, was the one the world wanted to see. Could Johnson pull off the double against a field that included Ato Boldon from Trinidad and Tobago and Frankie Fredericks from Namibia?

Before the gun, before the flashbulbs lit up the night, before the roars, four thoughts ran on a loop in Johnson's mind:

Keep my head down.

Pump my arms.

Explode.

I'm a bullet.

Michael is one of my closest friends. We have presented together at many speaking events, and there has never been a time I have been around him and not gotten better. Michael has his own statue at Nike headquarters. He is a no-bullshit competitor, and his mind made his God-given talent even better. It took visualizing to help make Michael the very best in the world.

I met Michael in 2001, five years after he smoked the field in the 200 in Atlanta, when he visited IMG Academy to talk to a group of NFL draft prospects about speed. This group included TCU tailback LaDainian Tomlinson, who would enter the Pro Football Hall of Fame in 2017. It also included Purdue quarterback Drew Brees and Michigan offensive lineman Steve Hutchinson, who will both get into the Hall of Fame as soon as they're eligible. These guys wanted to hear Michael talk about gold medals and tell them how to run blazing forty-yard-dash times at the NFL combine. Instead, Michael gave them something infinitely more valuable. He gave them the secrets of a champion. He told them that if they wanted to be great, they had fewer choices than they realized. He advised them to think neutrally, even though none of us had thought to call it neutral thinking yet. He also showed them how to visualize their successes before they happened using neutral statements that reminded them of all they'd done to prepare.

Keep my head down. Pump my arms. Explode. I'm a bullet. Michael called this the "danger zone," and he told me he created it out of necessity. He drew lane eight in Olympic qualifying in 1992, and he realized that his own mind would have to manufacture a new strategy because he wouldn't have the benefit of seeing his top competitors on either side as he traditionally had in lane three or four. If they weren't in his field of vision, he couldn't really run the race against them. So he visualized what it would take to win the race, and based on his own practice performances leading up to qualifying he created reminders that would make him the best he could be if he followed his own instructions. The technique worked so well that Michael used it in every race he ran afterward. Unfortunately, it couldn't help him in the 1992 Olympics in Barcelona.

Two weeks before those Olympics, Michael contracted food poisoning. It wrecked his training, and he didn't even make the final. The mind was willing, but the body wasn't. "You don't know if you're ever going to get this opportunity again," Michael told me later. "That is the nature of being an Olympic athlete. You've got to perform on the day."

When he prepared for the 1996 Olympics, Michael treated every run in every practice for what it was—a chance to get a little bit better. He attacked his training with the idea that the 400 and the 200 in 1996 might be his final chances at Olympic gold. (They weren't, but he had no way of knowing that.) "I had to ask myself: 'Am I willing to do this?' And I said, 'Okay, I'm willing to do this,'" Michael told those draft prospects. "You've got to be realistic in setting your goals and then figure out if you're willing to make the sacrifices in order to do it. Then you have to figure out a plan to go about achieving the goal."

Michael told those football players to write down their plans as they would a list before they went to the grocery store. Don't write it down, and pay the price. Write it down, and help yourself minimize anxiety and simplify your mission. This is how words connect to visualization. As we read it enters the frontal cortex and we see it in our mind and experience it emotionally even though we aren't physically doing it. Maxwell Maltz, a surgeon who became a pioneer in the self-help field in the 1960s, called this psycho-cybernetics and taught people to use it to help their self-image. Nick Saban calls it a part of "The Process"—his system of teaching that prioritizes an unbiased look at the steps required to meet any goal. To me, it's one of those choices that isn't really a choice. Structure your vision and imprint a road map for future outcomes. If you don't, you leave too much up to chance. The nights before the national title games that ended the 2009, 2011, 2012, 2013, 2015, and 2017 college football seasons, I sat with the quarterbacks of the teams I worked for. We would watch video and review and discuss exactly what neutral thoughts connected to the type of performance we would need for the next day. Like Michael had his list, we would have a simple plan that I would reinforce with a text message in the morning or before the game. I'd usually include a picture I had taken at the stadium the day before so they could visualize the place where they'd need to execute the behaviors we'd discussed. I held similar meetings and sent similar texts to NFL hopefuls about to run the 40-yard dash at the combine in Indianapolis. That run, which takes less than five seconds, can make a player millions of extra dollars. It can also cost him millions of dollars. So he needs to make that successful run in his mind before he runs for the NFL scouts and executives. Why? It takes visualization to see an outcome in advance of it ever happening. And the best imagery comes from the inside out.

Michael's plan required visualizing every aspect of the races that would lead to gold medals. That meant *every* aspect—from his head to his feet. Michael left himself no choice for the 1996 Olympics after a meeting with his team at Nike. About a year before the Olympics, Nike designer Tobie Hatfield showed Michael and his coach a prototype of the shoe Michael would wear. "It was never about the color of the shoes," Michael said. "The idea was to make the most technologically advanced, lightest track spike ever." The prototype wasn't gold. It had a mirrored finish. Michael told Hatfield not to change a thing. Michael's coach disagreed. "With 100,000 people sitting in the stands, it's going to look like a regular silver shoe," he said. Reflexively, Michael asked, "Tobie, can you make that in gold?"

"His jaw just dropped," Michael said. "Like, 'Are you seriously considering gold shoes?'" Michael swears he never thought about how awkward it would look if he won bronze in gold shoes. "But that was my mindset," Michael said. "I wasn't going there for anything else. I wasn't training for anything else." By the time he was on the track in Atlanta, Michael knew what would happen.

"Imagine you're standing behind the blocks and the ultimate prize is there within reach and you're about to have the opportunity to grab it," he said. "In the next nineteen seconds, you're going to know whether you're successful or not. It comes down to two things:

Are you prepared?

Can you execute?

"There's a yes-or-no answer to those. Either you are and you can, or you aren't and you can't."

Michael knew the answer was yes because he had visualized everything that needed to happen and had taken all the steps required during his preparation to make sure he could turn that vision into reality.

"Back up six months or a year," he said. "If you're not prepared, you're going to wish you'd taken those opportunities on those days that you didn't do everything you were supposed to do because that wasn't the priority and something else was. You're going to wish you had made a different choice."

When the starter's gun fired, Michael didn't have to wonder. Years after the race, Boldon would tell SB Nation that he'd consulted a psychic who predicted "glory for Ato" in the 200. As Boldon rounded the curve, he was still ahead of Michael. Then it happened. Michael zoomed past. All Boldon saw were those gold shoes flashing with each step. Michael finished in 19.32 seconds, shattering the world record at the time. A psychic's guess was no match for the combination of visualization, neutral thinking, and great choices.

It's important to remember that we're not talking about fantasies. If you can't run fast, visualizing winning Olympic gold in the 200 meters won't help you do it. But in your area of expertise at work or in your daily life, you can always visualize the steps to better outcomes. The key is neutral imagery. Neutral imagery can be in a statement of who we are or in a statement of behaviors. The words trigger the pictures, which affect the emotions. Before our under-17 or under-20 national soccer teams would leave for World Cup qualifying or the World Cup itself, I'd take the players to the beach. They would sit around a fire and listen to the crackling of the flames and the lapping of the water on the shore. I'd take them through a process called progressive muscle relaxation.

We'd breathe in for four seconds, hold it for four seconds, and release it for four seconds. We'd then flex a series of muscles for four seconds and release for four seconds, working from our toes to our face. After that I'd tell each player to see themselves as the first person walking off the bus in the designated World Cup city. Then they'd imagine themselves in the locker room preparing for the game. Then I'd tell them to visualize walking into the stadium. At this point, I'd play the World Cup theme music with crowd noise added in and then fade it to the announcement, "PLEASE RISE FOR THE NATIONAL ANTHEM OF THE UNITED

STATES OF AMERICA." I could see the emotions on our
players' faces. In that moment, they were in the stadium.
After this, I'd give them ten minutes to envision their
role in the game before bringing them back. Walking off
the beach those evenings, the quiet sense of urgency was
palpable. Every week these young players had exposure to
psychological fundamentals. The guided neutral imagery
would be our key finale. We'd put the crowd noise and
theme music and national anthem announcement on
each of their devices so they could include these in their
playlists. Seeing where you want to go in advance doesn't
get you there. I concede that. But I believe in the aggregate
of marginal gains. It's a piece that helps. I can tell you this
with absolute certainty: seeing nothing doesn't get you
anywhere, anytime, in any environment, any place.

Neutral words can also help you visualize what you want.
Michael Johnson created his words to describe what he'd
do in his ideal race performance. They weren't unrealistic.
They weren't fantasies. They were actions, behaviors, and
feelings that Michael could enact because of his preparation.

Keep my head down.

Pump my arms.

Explode.

I'm a bullet.

I've worked with college football teams that chose their own neutral statements based on words they felt described the personality of the team. When I worked with Michigan's football team in 2014, I made a list of words that I felt described what the coaches and players were trying to achieve:

- able
- accepting
- adventurous
- aggressive
- ambitious
- athletic
- beast mode
- bold
- brave
- bright
- calm
- caring
- committed
- confident
- considerate
- cooperative
- courageous
- creative
- daring
- demanding
- detailed
- determined

- devout
- dominant
- driven
- efficient
- elite
- energetic
- enthusiastic
- excited
- expert
- explosive
- faithful
- fighter
- forgiving
- generous
- giving
- gracious
- hardworking
- helpful
- honest
- humble
- intelligent
- inventive
- kind
- knowledgeable
- leader
- loyal
- lunch-pail mentality
- mature
- patient
- proud

- quick
- reliable
- respectful
- responsible
- reverent
- self-confident
- sensible
- serious
- smart
- stable

- strong
- studious
- successful
- talented
- thoughtful
- tireless
- tolerant
- trusting
- unselfish
- unstoppable

I then told the players to each choose their top five. I tallied the votes, and we used the top vote-getters to form a team affirmation that also served as a mission statement: "We clock in. We attack and DOMINATE in all areas of our lives consistently. We lead by example and understand that preparation is the key to our success. We have unity, not uniformity, and understand our individual talents are part of the overall goal to be our absolute best. Nothing happens by accident. Our offense is aggressive. We play to win. We attack. Our defense is unrelenting. We will hit you. Then do it again. Teams FEEL what it's like to compete against Michigan. Our special teams are play-makers. One rep. One mentality. YOU'VE got to earn everything against TEAM 135. We defend our home and EMBRACE battles on the road. BRING IT ON. We uphold the Michigan standard and ADD to it. IT'S our time. IT'S our responsibility."

Everyone's affirmation will be different. Sometimes our words will change. In 2018, Michael Johnson faced another foe. *I'm a bullet* wasn't going to help him win this race, but all the mental skills he had acquired as an elite athlete would.

That September, Michael had just finished a workout when he felt tingling down his left arm and side. He went to the hospital, where he nearly fell off the table because his left leg didn't work. Doctors told Michael he'd had a transient ischemic attack, more commonly known as a ministroke. They told Michael he would probably regain the use of his leg, but he'd have to work at it. So Michael, who was fifty-one at the time, slipped back into the Olympic mindset. "I've got the opportunity to get back to who I was, back to 100 percent," he said of his thought process at the time. "There's nothing more important than that. Do I want to do it? No. But I'm going to do it."

Two days after the attack, Michael found himself at another kind of starting line as he started rehab. The distance?

About 200 meters. Using a walker, it took ten to fifteen minutes to traverse what once took him 19.32 seconds. "I'm walking and my therapist is trying to help coordinate my left leg," Michael said. "I can feel with every step getting a tiny fraction closer to what I'm doing on the right—but still a lifetime away."

It wouldn't take a lifetime, though. Michael had reentered the mode that won him his gold medals. "I was feeling that little bit of improvement," he said. "I know what that feels like. I've been there." In his racing days, Michael worked days at a time for incremental gains. Shaving off a few hundredths of a second sometimes took months. So Michael's brain inherently accepted the idea that while he wouldn't walk normally again overnight, he would walk normally again if he worked at it. The tiny improvements he felt that first day helped him visualize the bigger gains that would come later. The goal in rehab was to retrain Michael's left leg to work like his right leg did. Once he made the choice that walking normally again was his priority, nothing could stop him. "I will make a full recovery," Michael told himself. "And I'm going to do it faster than everybody else."

Doctors indeed marveled at Michael's progress. He did walk normally again within a few months, much sooner than most people in the same situation. He made a plan to recover, and he visualized the literal steps he'd have to take to get back to walking normally. As he made progress, he visualized the next, bigger steps. His visions kept coming true until eventually he reached his ultimate goal.

There is effectively zero chance that you'll run for gold at the Olympics. But there is a decent chance that one day you'll find yourself standing next to a physical therapist trying to make something work again. You don't need to be Michael Johnson in that moment. You just need to choose his mentality.

Your mind matters. You exert incredible influence on what you think. What you see. We don't have to accept life the way it comes to us. We can design it in advance so we can get the life we seek.

8

It Takes Self-Awareness

The criminal truth in sports as it relates to psychological growth is that the front office, administration, and coaches believe that success only happens by selecting the right player. If they don't get the right guy through the draft or free agency in the pros or through recruiting or transfers in college, they missed. Eventually that player gets discarded and they try again with someone else. If a player gets into a building with a contract and needs any bandwidth to go from great to greater or good to better or struggling to functional, the majority of teams are fucked. That's the truth. They know it. The Jacksonville Jaguars were willing to try something new when they hired me and Chad Bohling in 2002.

There was no external impetus for the Jags to hire us. But a full staff of coaches knew the team's best chances rode on the healthy legs of tailback Fred Taylor, and they were willing to try something different because they knew Fred was special. They just couldn't figure out how to keep him healthy. In a league where wins are the EBITDA and losses make you unemployed, it takes what it takes. Mike Ryan, the Jags' director of sports medicine, would be a catalyst in my career. He suggested that Jaguars coach Tom Coughlin meet with us. That's how we wound up in front of Coughlin hearing the sentence that seems to pop up so often in my career: "You've got four minutes." We turned that four minutes into an hour, and Coughlin gave us a shot. But there really wasn't much risk. The Jaguars needed to get the most out of Fred, who had a rare blend of size and speed that simply couldn't be replaced through the draft or free agency. This left the organization more open to new ideas than others might have been.

When we started work with the team, Chad and I knew Fred was both the focus and the real opportunity. In our early conversations with Fred, he made his mission clear:

Play sixteen games.

Play one full season. It was that simple. In your world, this may mean going an entire year without a sick day or exercising five days a week for a month. Identifying the goal is critical, because something vague and open-ended like "don't miss work" or "exercise a lot" or—in Fred's case— "stay healthy" feels insurmountable. Putting a number on the goal gives your mind a place to focus. That doesn't make reaching the goal any easier. It isn't easy. And people aren't trying to steamroll your ass into a desk drawer every minute. So imagine how this felt for Fred.

As we started this journey with Fred, we recognized just how critical behaviors would be to unlocking his incredible gifts. And they were truly incredible. Fred is six feet tall. He weighed 228 pounds at his pro day at the University of Florida in March 1998. Most backs that big tend to lumber with the ball, using their strength to drag tacklers an extra yard or two. Fred could do that, but he also could turn on the afterburners and outrun an entire defense. At that pro day, the scouts' stopwatches clocked Fred somewhere between 4.31 and 4.39 seconds in the 40-yard dash. That would be blazing for a guy thirty pounds lighter. For someone as big as Fred, it was exceptionally rare.

That run vaulted Fred into the top half of the first round of the NFL draft. Jacksonville selected him with the ninth overall pick and gave him a six-year contract that included a $5 million signing bonus. I know this sounds like peanuts compared to salaries today, but at the time that was the biggest signing bonus a draftee had gotten in three years. Fred made the Jags look smart for choosing him. In fifteen games as a rookie, he gained 1,223 yards. But he would play only ten games in 1999 because of a hamstring injury and thirteen games in 2000 because of a knee injury. In 2001, he played only two games and carried the ball only thirty

times. That thirtieth carry came in the second quarter of
a game against the Tennessee Titans. Fred took a handoff
from Mark Brunell and made a great jump cut to get past
the line of scrimmage. He ran for a few yards and tried to
cut again. When he did, he dropped the ball on the ground
and collapsed. On the TV broadcast, you could see a wave
of pain on Fred's face just before he dropped the ball. "That
is the most pain I ever had," Fred said of the injury. That's
because his groin muscle had torn off the bone. He was
done for the year. Meanwhile, he'd developed a frustrating
nickname: Fragile Fred.

Chad and I were hired to help Fred find a way to make it
through the next season. There was no magic pill. Breathing
wouldn't fix this. No magical mantra would either. We
had to help him understand the path and the formula to
get back to the greatness that made him dominate the SEC
and his first year in the NFL (just ask Bobby Bowden or
Dan Marino). But at first, he didn't trust us. Though he
has a great relationship with Coughlin now, at the time he
was wary of the organization because when Coughlin was
asked by reporters during the 2001 season when Fred was
coming back, Coughlin insinuated that Fred should already
be back. But the injury was serious, and Fred felt as if
Coughlin had thrown him under the bus. Since Coughlin
had okayed hiring me, Chad and I had to be the enemy.
Fred was *us*. We were *them*. He thought we'd been planted
by management to brainwash him. At first, he wouldn't
open up at all.

Gradually, Chad and I gained Fred's trust by proving we were interested only in his well-being. We didn't want to report what he told us to the coaching staff or the front office. We wanted to help him be the best football player he could be. Later Fred would say that somewhere in the middle of our journey I went from being someone management hired to being a real friend. He got comfortable with me; I got comfortable with him. He could open up to me knowing I wasn't going to rat him out to Coughlin. I was only going to use the information to help him.

Once Fred started talking, we had a chance to make real progress. Early on, we'd go through a simple chart that my father had shared with me. It was built on western Asian philosophy. People can live in one of four states:

Unconsciously incompetent: we don't know, and we don't know that we don't know.

Consciously incompetent: we know that we don't know.

Unconsciously competent: we don't know that we know.

Consciously competent: we know, and we know that we know (and therefore can repeat it).

If these terms look familiar to you, then you may be saying "Wait—isn't unconsciously competent supposed to be the most enlightened state?" That's how Martin Broadwell described it in 1969 when writing about teachers.[1] To Broadwell, a person reached the highest level when they had practiced the required skills so extensively that performing those skills well essentially came down to muscle memory.

My dad looked at it differently, and I agree with him. We are at our best not only when our instincts are practiced and sound, but when we fully understand *why* we're successful or unsuccessful. In the sports world, unconscious competence describes an athlete or coach who has an abundance of natural ability but without any idea of how to properly harness that ability. This person may succeed but may have no idea how to repeat that success. In sports, conscious competence makes more sense as the most enlightened state.

Fred clearly understood he was in the third category. He knew how to produce an incredible performance, but he had been reckless with his body. He didn't yet understand how to optimize it. We wondered who was in the Jags' building who *did* understand. We set out to find some consciously competent guys working alongside Fred whom he could use as examples for the behaviors he would need to adopt. We asked the Jags' staff which players had made it to their second and third contracts, where the real money is in the NFL. Those were the guys Fred needed to emulate. Think about all that stands between a player and a second contract:

- He must stay healthy in a sport where the collisions carry the same force as car crashes.

- Not only must he perform well enough to be one of the best handful of players in the world at his position, but he must also be so superior that his team is willing to pay for him rather than for a slightly less skilled but much cheaper option.

As we observed the Jags who were playing on second and third contracts, we noticed two things all of them had in common:

1. They arrived each morning around 6:30.

2. They ended each day with some form of an ice bath.

Each of the second- and third-contract players had his own habits, techniques, and tricks, but these seemed to be the ones that were the clear common denominators.

Longevity was the goal. Fred may not have known it at the time, but the formula to play all sixteen games in the NFL wasn't much different from the formula to play more than that. Safety Roy Williams, one of the nearly 400 NFL draft prospects I'd have the opportunity to meet and work with over the years, told me that he knew his "body was his moneymaker" and that it was on him to keep that "bank" writing checks. I loved that. And if we have ten times the influence on ourselves that others do and up to another multiple of seven on top of that if it's negative—in thought, language, or behavior—then what happens to our bodies is in our hands.

But Fred wasn't doing the things the guys on their second and third contracts did. He wasn't taking care of his body. He was, as he calls it, "hanging out excessively." Staying out late and doing the things one does when staying out late led to insufficient hydration. Insufficient hydration led to minor soft tissue injuries. Those nagging injuries, when combined with a running style that Fred compared to "going 150 mph all the time," led to major injuries. To make matters worse, Fred grew frustrated because he had developed a reputation as someone who couldn't stay healthy.

In spite of his gifts, Fred felt helpless. His success seemed to occur from the outside in, instead of being something he created from the inside out. Helplessness is a state that can be quickly followed by a much deeper and scarier place: hopelessness. If you don't become helpless, then you won't become hopeless. And if we could help Fred stop feeling helpless, he'd never be in danger of becoming hopeless. Fred would get down on himself. He never doubted his ability, but he wondered why he was the one who had to get hurt. And then someone would call him Fragile Fred in the newspaper or on the radio, and he'd add anger to his despair. After a while, the anger became Fred's defining trait. He still knew he could run the football better than anyone. But the frustration of being stuck on the sidelines because of those frequent injuries caused that anger to boil inside him.

It has been truly inspiring to have a front-row seat to watch these athletes, teams, and coaches unlock these incredible secrets right in front of me. You never really know what is going to cause the breakthrough. Each situation has its own history and circumstances. But when they get it, it's like a brake being released. They reach maximum velocity quickly. With the Florida State Seminoles in 2013, we would watch *Lone Survivor* the night before playing Clemson at home in Death Valley. The players would walk out of that theater in South Carolina changed, and they would roll to a 51–14 win the next night. In 2007 with the US national soccer team, it was a beach event where every player would speak and we'd listen to the national anthem as a group with our feet in the water and the fire behind us late in the evening. As I walked off that beach in Bradenton with a young Jozy Altidore and Freddy Adu, I could see in the eyes of those two and many others that they had this sense and understanding of what the idea of "team" was all about. With Georgia's football team in 2017, in a quiet team room we would do an activity (developed eighteen years earlier with an under-17 girls' soccer team in Boca Raton) where our fifteen leaders would identify their responsibilities on two lines at the top of a piece of paper. They would then pass their paper to the right and receive the paper from their teammate on the left. Then they would write two

sentences with *their* thoughts about the responsibilities of
the player whose name was at the top of the page. Then
they'd pass the pages again and repeat the exercise. By the
end, they would receive a 360-degree perspective on what
their teammates believed their role to be. The weight they
would carry within the team became more clearly defined.
The expectations of their teammates became clearer to
each player. Looking at those players' faces, it was obvious
they wanted that accountability. Those young men chose a
different path because they became consciously competent.
In 2007, I sat with Florida State women's soccer coach Mark
Krikorian the night before his team played Connecticut
with a trip to college soccer's version of the Final Four on
the line. His players shared exactly what it would take for
them and their teammates to win. And they were right.
That team did go to the final four, and I found myself in the
middle of a dog pile!

A young Russell Wilson said at our first meeting, "I want
to know what you know. I want to know what Drew
Brees did. I don't want to leave here—this magical place in
Bradenton—feeling that I haven't done everything I can.
That I haven't learned everything I could learn. I'd like
you to hold me to that, Trev. I know you've been there. I
did my homework on you. I did my homework on Chris
Weinke. My agent and I both did. That's why we're here." I
didn't see the Super Bowls for him then, but I heard it. The
puzzle pieces were beginning to fit together. Not because
of outside forces, but because of Russell. The same was

true for Jozy. For the FSU football team. For the Georgia football team. They were helping themselves by learning and understanding. There's little information that is not already out there. It's there for all of us, if we are there to receive it. A great program or organization provides and adapts that formula on the front end. They adapt. They trust. An individual is truly in control of the individual. No one else is. There are speed limits. There are rules. But there's a clear path to a version of success in most every situation. These are relative and based on the situation, but if you know yourself, if you are consciously competent, you can create the behaviors that allow you to produce the best possible outcome. This applies to losing, to winning, to business, to bankruptcy, to marriage, to divorce. It applies to everything.

So many of us are dominated by our state of mind. Our moods. Our feelings. And like Fred Taylor in his early career, both good days and bad days can confuse us. Everything seems to be happening to us and around us, not within us or for us.

When you identify what that ideal recipe is for you, and why that particular day or week or quarter worked for you or that movie emboldened your team or that event brought everyone together, you begin to control your own formula. You start to give credit to a specific set of behaviors and not to something external. It's like when you learn to cook instead of just eating what is put in front of you.

Fred learned that in 2002. He started arriving at the complex between 6:00 and 6:30 a.m. Upon arrival, he'd go through a maintenance routine with his trainer—stretching and preparing his body for the day. He originally planned to do this routine three days a week, but quickly decided to do it every day he came to the complex. To make it in so early, Fred began going to bed earlier. He didn't hang out excessively. Therefore, he didn't show up to the complex dehydrated. His days ended in ice baths. Suddenly, the nagging soft tissue injuries were reduced. And the minor injuries he had healed more quickly because of his willingness to prep his body and ice it down every day. A few years into our time together, I showed Fred a quote that really resonated with him. It was from Norman Vincent Peale. Peale wrote *The Power of Positive Thinking*, but he could think neutrally with the best of them.

> Give every bit of yourself. Hold nothing back. Life cannot deny itself to the person who gives life his all.[2]

Fred had become willing to give every bit of himself to attain his goal. "There's a thin line," Fred said. "Routine looks like commitment. But commitment reinforces the routine." Fred had become consciously competent. He had learned what his body needed, and with our help he developed the routines necessary to keep his body functioning properly. As he said, he did this because he had committed to the idea of playing sixteen games that season. If he wanted to do that, he didn't really have a choice. It

takes what it takes. Fred didn't play just one full sixteen-
game season. After he started working with us, he played
forty-six consecutive games before the next one he missed
because of an injury. Fred wound up playing thirteen
NFL seasons, rushing for 11,695 yards. He ran for sixty-
six touchdowns and caught eight more. "Trevor and Chad
didn't just save my career," Fred said. "They saved my life. I
learned how to cope and move forward."

As Fred would make the decision to behave like a player
who would play all sixteen games, that set of behaviors
backed by his gifts would then allow him to feel helpful
to himself. And helpful is a precursor to hopeful. I believe
that hope is one of the most incredible medicines of all. But
it is different from faith. It doesn't count on you to believe
something that you've never seen. You contribute to your
own sense of hopefulness.

Fred would win the Ed Block Courage Award from the team
after our first year with him. He would say that of all the
accolades he received, he was most proud of that. But the
courage was not so much about the thousands of yards he'd
run for. Or the safety who had challenged his greatness in
the media and whom he would then flatten to beat Peyton
Manning and the Colts late in that season to get a critical
victory in front of a prime-time audience. Or the forty-six
consecutive games he'd play after he let us into his life and
we were lucky enough to have him be a part of ours. The
real courage he showed was his willingness to talk to a

twenty-six- and twenty-eight-year-old every week. He was willing to listen to us so he could be his best. For the first few years, Fred, Chad, and I were all problem solvers and solution finders for Fred's gifts. After Chad moved on to work with the New York Yankees, the last five years would be just Fred and me. Fred would commit to meet with me every week for eight years until he left for New England. Fred retired a consciously competent football player, a consciously competent father, a consciously competent businessman, and an incredible leader in the Jacksonville community. He "behaved" himself into this person.

This happened intentionally, and it wasn't easy. Many conversations were challenges. Challenging him to live up to the incredible gifts he'd been given. To lead others when his own body was broken. To be his very best when his mind was tired and his baby was teething. To be an All-Pro when he had to manage life on top of football and on top of the expectations of Nike, of his hometown of Belle Glade, and of himself and his past greatness. "Right now, people are just calling it positive energy," Fred said. "I've been doing that since 2002."

Fred had to learn more about himself to develop the behaviors that ultimately helped him reach his goal. He also had to learn why the people who had already achieved his goal had succeeded. That way, he could emulate them and use the knowledge of himself to create behaviors that led to full, sixteen-game seasons. You may not want to play a full NFL season, but you can use the same techniques to help you reach goals in your own life. This process is not finite. It isn't for Fred. It isn't for you. Fred was willing to study his teammates and learn what worked for them. Then he tried it on himself and learned what worked for him. But even after he became consciously competent, he kept learning about himself and kept adapting. Self-awareness is critical, but we also must understand that we change as our circumstances change. We have to keep assessing ourselves honestly so we can stay self-aware as our lives evolve.

We ultimately will be defined by our next decision, our next motion, our next behavior. Good or bad. That shift in understanding changed Fred Taylor's life. Take showing up in the training room at 6:30 a.m. I still remember him asking, "What will I do getting in there so early?" At first the answer was "Who the fuck knows, bro? But there must be something that the other guys who get there early do." And there was. Those players who were playing on second and third contracts and making generational money were in there preparing their bodies for the pounding to come. And by setting their alarms early, they gave themselves no option to stay out too late the night before or to get drunk (which would have dehydrated them). For them, there was no choice. They wanted to keep playing, to keep earning that money. So they adapted their behaviors to ensure they did. Fred saw that, and then he did it. His mentality is as responsible for his success today as it was for the thousands of rushing yards at sports' highest level. The only real

momentum we have is what we learn about what produced
our success or what created the adversity that challenges us.
It is understanding our current level of competence. That's
the first step. That understanding, even in the absence of
action, can become life changing. And it's not limited to
elite athletes. You face challenges that can be overcome by
continuously learning about yourself. I do too.

If you think those people you watch on TV aren't living
what you're living, you're wrong. They are. Behind their
Instagram pages, life is hard. This is no different for me.
I can't talk about the millions of dollars I earned as a self-
made guru, because I don't have that. I don't own an island.
I have yet to do 16,000 pull-ups. I'm relearning how to
meet people. I don't wake up at 4:00 a.m. or eat kale every
day. But I do compete, and I don't quit, and I refuse to give
up on myself. I share that characteristic with many of the
people and organizations I have the privilege of serving.
I choose this. This choice structure has never mattered
more for me than right now or last year.

Last year was difficult. As I drove through the streets of
Seekonk, Massachusetts, in June 2018, I felt numb. I was
by myself, and that had become an all-too-frequent reality
for me. Feeling alone doesn't always require the absence
of people. I was around a lot of people. Loneliness is
something deeper. It's not independence. It's disconnection.
Disconnection has been given a hero's title for professionals
in this era; it's referred to now as compartmentalization.

I was a beast at this. Many of the best are. But this comes
with consequences. I had finished seventeen consecutive
days working in seven states. I was trying to launch
multiple businesses. I was swimming in a deeper end than
I had before—with no lifeguard. I had no big company
backing me. For the first time every contract was up for
renewal in the same four-week window. Negotiating new
deals to replace four expiring ones is as exciting as it
sounds. I was in New York for work and flew to Providence,
Rhode Island, early one morning. It was my final stop of
this trip, and it would be the toughest.

I pulled into the beautiful new Herren Wellness treatment
center, and in moments I would put my arms around
longtime friend Chris Herren. Chris was one of the best
high school basketball players in Massachusetts history,
and he turned down scholarship offers from Kentucky
and Duke to stay near home and play at Boston College.
At BC, he got into cocaine. He left BC and transferred to
Fresno State, where he played well but had to go to rehab
after testing positive for drugs. Chris was drafted in the
second round by the NBA's Denver Nuggets, and he was
introduced to OxyContin while playing for the team as a
rookie. Chris got sent home to play for the Boston Celtics
before his second season, but he got cut after only a year.
So he went to Europe, and his Oxy addiction went with
him. By 2004 he was using heroin. Chris got arrested in
December of that year when police found him unconscious
in a Dunkin' Donuts drive-through in Portsmouth, Rhode

Island. They also found eighteen packets with heroin residue and the paraphernalia required to use heroin.

In June 2008, Chris was still using heroin and drinking heavily when he crashed his car into a telephone pole in Fall River, Massachusetts. After that incident, some very kind people helped Chris get his life back together. Former NBA star Chris Mullin paid for Chris to go to an intensive rehab facility in New York. He then moved to a three-month program. He emerged drug-free, and since then he has dedicated his life to helping others beat addiction.

Chris and I were close. I had called him many years ago and invited him to both Alabama and FSU. I knew he could be a game changer for those organizations. And he was. He still is. But now I needed him. Both he and Ryan Leaf had both shown up big for me. Remember Ryan Leaf? In 1998 Ryan was a star quarterback coming out of Washington State, and there was an intense debate for months about whether Ryan or Tennessee's Peyton Manning should go number one in the NFL draft. Looking back, it was a no-brainer. Peyton became one of the best QBs who ever played in the NFL. Ryan, who went number two, flamed out after only a few years. Ryan struggled with addiction for years in his post-NFL life. He went to jail. He hit rock bottom multiple times. But he also got clean, and now he also has dedicated his time to helping others.

Chris and Ryan are uniquely polarizing figures in sports who became redefined by their ability to leverage a

challenging past to create an incredible present. I am
grateful to both. Chris and I were in his treatment center
on this gray June day, and I was coming to visit someone
of significant value to me, someone I had a complex
relationship with. It was rough. When I drove out hours
later, I realized my emotions were drowning me. Everything
that had seemed so solid and strong in my life had folded.
Why? And it all had happened at the same time. Why? I
would also be forced to spend well into the six figures on
things that seemingly had nothing to do with me. Why?
This also coincided with my strategic decision to pull back
from sports and say no to guaranteed opportunities in order
to open up more time and move into the business world.
That June, I doubted every bit of that decision.

The summary: Money? Fucked. Business? Challenged.
Relationships? Lost. In June 2018, this was my truth. I
knew it. I felt far from being a fucking guru. But I also
knew, just like Fred did in 2002, that I was not built to stay
here. None of us are. Russell and I end every text to one
another with four words: *the best is ahead.* That could be
my truth. It *could* be. I had the answers, but I needed to be
open to listening. I needed to get aligned with behaviors
that could get me where I wanted to be.

I believe your destiny is defined by what you do next. It's
okay if you believe something external moved you to do it,
but you still have to do it. No one can live your life for you.
Maybe they can live it through you, in some way, but the

doing is still up to you. That's what this book is all about. It's not a free pass on your past. You are responsible for that. All of it—the great parts and the parts that fell short. But it's what's next that matters, not what was. What's next is the only thing you can still influence. Accept that basic fact, and life moves quickly to what's next. And you'll think a lot fucking less about what was. Athletes get this. During games, good cornerbacks don't think about the touchdowns they've allowed. They think about the next play. Coaches get it too. The best don't dwell on the play calls that didn't work. They worry about what might work on the next drive. That last game is over. That last play is over. There's no debating it. If you won, why? If you didn't, why not? At this point in my life, I wasn't winning much. In truth, I was consciously incompetent in way too many areas. I knew that I didn't know what to do next. But at least I knew I didn't know. As nuts as that sounds, that mattered. After hugging Chris and leaving Rhode Island, I flew to Los Angeles. I landed and drove late at night to Occidental College. I ran the same hills I ran as a college athlete. Why did I choose those hills to run? I don't know. My guess? Because I had succeeded there. Perhaps I needed the reminder that I was actually as strong and physically fit as I was then. And after my sixth lap up the hills, I stopped at the top and took out a pen and a flashlight and began working my way into conscious competence.

I had to identify what my version of "play a sixteen-game season" would look like and why I was experiencing life's version of an injury right now. The answers weren't easy, but I had started. Life rewards those who start. *Just do it* works. Doing the work works. As I was writing on that hill, out of the blue I got a text from Russell. He wrote,

Never forget Trev. You're a King. YOU ARE A KING.

Why he sent that at that time I'll never know. But it mattered, and I needed it. I made a decision that night to behave like royalty. That decision moved me forward.

This is what I wrote on that 53-degree night in LA:

IT'S what you do NOW that makes the difference. It may also be what you choose to STOP doing.

BUSINESS REALITIES

I chose a new path business-wise because I'd seen the outcomes of the old path. My fears and the discomfort are happening now because I'm right in the middle of the unknown. It's terrifying, but it is good. After terrifying is new, and new is where I need to be. Stay the course, because through this uncertainty was a path we had mapped out very carefully. Live what you teach.

Jim Lovell couldn't land on Earth when he was still near the moon. Fred Taylor would play one game in a row, forty-six times, and that's a process. I needed to live what I'd observed and taught.

SOCIAL REALITIES

Socially it's time to learn. You were strong before. You can be strong again. You hit a home run before. You can hit a home run again. Reach out to winners and relearn how to win. How to live. How to function. Choose connection over disconnection (where possible). You are not a cyborg. You are meant to live.

After leaving a spring-training speaking event in Florida the next year, I would grab an early dinner with an incredible woman who was down for a work event of her own. She would ask me a simple question that evening that really moved me: *Trev, who do you have on speed dial?* (Ironically, this is something Chris Herren had to ask himself when he woke up in an emergency room in 2008.) I smiled and pretended to answer, but in that moment I was exposed. I had no idea. But the question moved me toward finding that answer, and I can't thank my dinner companion enough for getting me to ask myself this question. That question led me to the simple truth: I needed to step up for myself in my life. I was my own answer. I needed to start helping myself by—as simplistic as this sounds—being helpful to myself. What an important lesson to remember.

There are times in our lives when we need to really count on ourselves. Too many of us operate on the principle of "if at first I don't succeed, set the blame quickly." That doesn't help us much in the long run. The relief is temporary. The challenges don't get conquered. We feel less equipped to manage a challenge after choosing the blame approach.

The SEALs say that you are never out of the fight. This applies to so much more than combat deployment. Conscious competence is knowing how to do what you need to do when you need to do it and why you are doing it. It gives us the ability to be dependable. To be consistent. To be reliable, both to ourselves and others. It is not, however, an individual pursuit. This competence doesn't mean you do everything on your own. "Knowing that you know" means you may activate key people, key behaviors, key locations, or key actions (to take or to not take) that help execute your process. You accept that. Part of Fred's competence was having Chad and me there as guardrails. We constantly worked to find different ways to help him discover and engage in his process. Success may not have been complicated, but it was far from easy. For years I've been given the privilege to help navigate this process with many of the best performers in the world. But part of my own competence in 2018 would be accepting short-term struggles and leaning into the emotions that drove better engagement and behaviors for me in my own life. The truth was that I wanted to be good at more than just my job. I wanted to be better at living my life.

Fred Taylor mastered his own process. It started by recognizing what wasn't working. We had to figure out why he wasn't staying healthy. It becomes a real weapon in your fight to know both what you need and how to find the people who can help you get it. When we choose dumb-ass behaviors, we choose failure. If we don't know our behaviors are dumb-ass, then we also make the choice not to know. You might think that the standard of performing in front of millions of people would drive quick alignment. But it's our own standards and behaviors that truly drive our process. We all have a set of behaviors that will make us successful. Whether or not we live them is the real question I hope you're asking yourself right now.

Start by looking around. Is there someone in the office who performs exceptionally well? Is there another parent at your child's school who always seems calm? Pay attention to their actions, to their habits. Or just ask them how they go about their day. This is useful information.

At the same time, seek out unbiased information about yourself. The page-passing exercise I described earlier is great even if you aren't an All-SEC linebacker. Gather your team at work or gather your friends and family. Each person starts with a piece of paper and writes their name at the top. They describe what they believe their responsibilities are in the organization or family unit or group. Then everyone passes their paper, receives a new one, and writes what they expect from the person named at the top of that paper. Keep passing until every person has written on every paper.

When you get your paper back, you'll have an honest
assessment of what is expected of you and what you're
currently contributing. From there you can identify areas
where you can improve. Knowing yourself can guide you in
forming the behaviors that will help you meet your goals.
Whether you're unconsciously incompetent, consciously
incompetent, or unconsciously competent, learning about
yourself and adjusting your behaviors can make you
consciously competent in every aspect of your life. That
won't make you as fast as Fred Taylor, but it'll make you
a happier, more productive employee, spouse, parent, or
whatever you dream of becoming.

9

It Takes Pressure

The world of high-level sports constantly asks you one question: Are you for real? You are asked it every practice, every meeting, and every time you stand toe-to-toe against someone who is basing their answer on how they fare against you. Everything is filmed. Every detail is scrutinized. Every moment is graded. Yes. Graded. Just like an academic exam. Your habits have no place to hide.

This happens on the practice field and in the locker room—before the TV networks, fan(atics), pregame shows, postgame shows, talk radio shows, family members, and agents enter the equation. You probably don't have those particular dynamics in your daily life, but you almost certainly have to deal with grading and scrutiny at work and at home. And your coworkers, your spouse, and your children are all asking—using different words—the same thing a football player's new teammate is asking him: Are you for real?

Whatever we're doing, we want the opportunity to contribute. To be held accountable. To be relevant. To be scared. To be emotional. To be fired. To be hired. To help others succeed and to succeed ourselves by doing so. In order to do this, you have to pay attention to your mind, your words, your behaviors, your responses, and your thinking. However you do it, it needs to be done. This is true anywhere, but it plays out more publicly in the world of sports.

On top of the obvious physiological requirements, there are knowledge requirements and interpersonal require-ments to function in a diverse, competitive-as-fuck envi-ronment. Think *Lord of the Flies*, but on a bigger island with much scarier opponents. And everyone needs that conch. Greatness is available to anyone—including your opponents—and the pressure is on you to snatch it first. This is true on the field, on the court, or in your office. You may be intimidated by that pressure you feel to per-form every day. Instead, try embracing it. Pressure isn't a burden. It isn't something to be avoided or minimized. As tennis great Billie Jean King said, pressure is a privilege. What does that mean? If you're under pressure, it means someone gives a shit what you do. If you're under pres-sure, it means someone relies on you. That is the ultimate privilege.

The key is responding properly to that pressure. Because
those who perform under the greatest pressure capture
the greatest victories. That's why you should run toward
pressure instead of away from it.

The world of sports is every bit as cutthroat as the business
Goldman Sachs operates. Goldman Sachs may drop the
bottom 5 to 10 percent of their workforce each year. That's
competitive, but sports pushes out far more. Twenty-one of
129 head coaching jobs in college football's top subdivision
turned over after the 2018 season. Six of thirty-two NFL
coaches got fired after the 2018 season. Every year, each of
those thirty-two teams brings ninety players into training
camp to compete for fifty-three jobs. That means 1,184
players will get fired before the first regular-season game. A
habit has no hiding place in sports. Good or bad. The film
will be watched. You will be graded. Your competency is
forced on you. You can't hide behind ignorance. You can't
say "I didn't know," because the team also has video of the
coach telling you the thing you were supposed to know. And
to anyone reading this, if you think you're hiding behind
ignorance in your non-sports job, you're not. You may not
have a "tell-the-truth Monday" with video in your office, but
that doesn't make the reality any different. It takes what it
takes in every walk of life. In your relationships—it takes
what it takes. With your health—it takes what it takes. To
get promoted—it takes what it takes. Average people become
average by doing average shit. It takes a specific set of
behaviors (or lack of them) to be average. No one is born

that way. People can behave themselves into mediocrity.
They also can behave themselves out of it. The right set
of behaviors doesn't guarantee wins. Embracing pressure
doesn't either. This still isn't about an outcome. It never will
be. It's about creating the opportunity to win by behaving
like people who win. It's about creating the opportunity
to succeed by not ignoring pressure when you know it's
a necessary challenge that anyone who achieves must
navigate. It's hard. You accept that.

I learned in year two at Alabama (2008) that psychological
strength needed to come from repetition. You can't hold
athletes accountable for an organizational language,
mentality, or mindset if you're not building the alphabet so
that they can spell and live the words. Alabama coach Nick
Saban and Texas A&M coach Jimbo Fisher believe this.
Kirby Smart at Georgia believes this. Most coaches and
leaders don't even know that they *don't* believe it. I work in
a field that doesn't really exist. I don't judge that. Coaches'
lack of interest in mental conditioning is probably due to the
seemingly infinite supply of willing employees. If athletes
are fucked up, you just discard them and get new ones.
If they're good, you're hoping they unlock the standard
to better. If they're great, most programs just try not to
fuck up their current ability rather than challenge them to
become even greater.

For eight weeks every summer at Alabama we'd execute
a program called Mindset: The Game Plan We Install for

Ourselves. A great program seeks feedback, and my time in the NFL and at Tuscaloosa with Coach Saban gave me the opportunity to give my opinion and suggest and implement ideas and changes as we'd evolve a new program. White papers weren't relevant. Practicality and effectiveness were.

I'd base much of this on the behaviorist theory in classic psychology. Behavioral psychology operates on a theory that humans adopt their behaviors because they are conditioned by their surroundings to choose those behaviors. Our behaviors, in essence, are a response to our environments.

A healthy self-esteem matters. To a football player or a concert pianist. Self-concept is real. Self-efficacy is real. Environmental self-image versus internal self-image? This is all real. Neutral didn't exist—at least not in my mind at that time—but we all knew negativity was a death sentence. All of these things matter because they are the building blocks that impact us daily for better or worse. Am I equipped to handle my life?

Mental conditioning isn't a part of how coaches are trained, so it isn't something that typically gets embedded in a program. That doesn't make the truth less true. Life is coming for us. Adversity is on a fucking steamroller headed right at us. Success? That can actually become its own adversity for many of the best. Everyone struggles with it. Coaches do. Front-office executives do. Certainly the players themselves do.

At the end of 2007, my belief was that the summer in college football nicely laid out a support program where we could give performers a set of psychological tools and team functionality to complement their strengths. Coach Saban trusted me to figure out a way to get this done.

By the time the Florida State team I worked with in 2013 hit the summer before the season, I had refined this program using five years of results at Alabama with Coach Saban and three years of results at Florida State with Coach Fisher. The Mindset program was customized for each team.

In that first meeting in the summer of 2013 at Florida State, I grabbed two whiteboards. Strength coaches Vic Viloria and Brandon "Red" Sanders helped me write down every result from 2011 and 2012 before we sat down with the players for the opening thirty-minute Mindset session. The room was quiet. I walked from the side of the theatre-style meeting room and stood to the side of the podium.

"Does anyone have anything to say about what they see on these boards up here? I recognize that they are the past. I know this summer and this time is about the future. But before we go to what's next—does anyone have something to say about what was?"

In the middle, leaning forward from the third row, senior linebacker Telvin Smith put his hand up. "I do, Trev," he said. He stepped over the three chairs in front of him, walked to me, and grabbed the pen out of my hand. In that moment, I realized he would become an incredible force multiplier for my summer responsibilities. I slowly made my way to the front row and sat on the far side. Telvin circled a series of games, then looked at the team.

"UVA at home," he said. "No more. NC State. No more. Wake Forest? Nah. No way. No more." Those were games Florida State had lost when the Seminoles had the more talented team.

I don't know what a Malcolm X speech was like to experience in person, but as someone who studied him in college I understood that he had a way about him that couldn't be taught. It both intimidated and inspired. Telvin had this, and the room was his.

"And why is this happening to us?" he asked his teammates. "They better? Those teams better?" He turned to center Bryan Stork. "What you think, Stork?" He looked at the presumed new starting quarterback, Jameis Winston. "How about you, Jameis?" He wheeled on defensive backs LaMarcus Joyner and Terrence Brooks. "Wake got something we don't have? We lose these games because of things we do. Things we don't do. I'm going to be real with you all. It ain't happening no more. I won't let it. Believe that. Here you go, Trev. Do what you do, because I know everyone's ass is going to listen. All summer."

I looked at Vic and Red. Wow. I grabbed the pen and opened with a video. The fourth quarter at Virginia Tech in 2012 appeared on the screen. It was 28 degrees—which may as well be Antarctica for a bunch of guys from Florida—but these guys did everything right and escaped Blacksburg with a 28–22 win. Then I showed the fourth quarter of the 2012 NC State game. Everything seemed to go wrong. They could connect the dots, and it reinforced Telvin's point.

At the end of the spring Jimbo Fisher had built a framework with the leaders around the idea of being elite. He had seeded much earlier what Telvin said that day, and our shirts and written materials were covered with the word *ELITE*. My job would be to help them see—across different sports and performers—examples of what that looked and sounded like. To build self-esteem we showed players what success looks like and how it's achieved, and we showed them that they had the capacity to do the same things. We also shared basic elements of how the mind processes and learns and is influenced. From the outside in and the inside out. There were no complicated words. Nothing was hard to grasp.

Over the coming weeks, players discussed the week in 2012 that led up to the NC State loss. They would compare their behaviors that week to their behaviors the week they played Virginia Tech. That allowed them to see their own influence on wins and losses before stepping onto the field. They opened up about specific guys doing or not doing things.

They were understanding and working out the idea of choice not really being a choice if they wanted to win. They were applying internal pressure to help themselves improve before the external pressure arrived. This is what the best organizations do. They create an atmosphere that prepares their people to handle the adversity they'll face in the course of the job. We were guiding players to simple truths, showing them that the path was clear and so were the requirements. In October of that year, those players would face real external pressure. Would their behaviors be good enough to allow them to embrace that pressure and capitalize on it?

When the Seminoles drove into Clemson, South Carolina, on October 19, 2013, it was time. We looked like the future. Clemson was the present. NFL scouts and famous alumni lined the field. This wasn't a game. It was *the* game.

Chris Fowler. Kirk Herbstreit. Lee Corso. David Pollack. Desmond Howard. ESPN's *College GameDay* spent three hours that morning hyping the matchup. Were we for real? Or were the Tigers? Both teams were about to get exposed.

Exposed is a neutral term in this case. You can be exposed as a fraud. You can also be exposed as a winner. The highest achievers—in sports, in business, in the military— actually embrace the opportunity to be exposed. Why? Because they've prepared for the moment. Who wants to live life on a practice field? At some point we need to step onto that real field and play. It's your choice. And there's that word again: choice.

"Streaks are meant to be broken," Jimbo said during his pregame interview, speaking of Florida State's five-game losing streak in Death Valley.

The game probably was over when Telvin—the linebacker who made my summer program so much easier—jarred the ball loose from Clemson's Stanton Seckinger on the Tigers' first play from scrimmage and Brooks recovered to give the Seminoles the ball at the Clemson 34-yard line. Two plays later, Winston threw a 22-yard touchdown pass to Kelvin Benjamin. It definitely was over midway through the second quarter when Winston hit Rashad Greene for a 72-yard touchdown pass that made the score 24-7. As Rashad reached the end zone, he put his finger to his lips. The crowd—which had made the stadium shake only an hour earlier—complied with silence. After Florida State's 51-14 win, Telvin approached receivers coach Lawrence Dawsey, who had played alongside Deion Sanders on some of the best teams Florida State ever produced. Was this what it felt like? Yes, Dawsey replied. With Telvin leading the way, that Florida State team had developed the behaviors champions adopt. Now the Seminoles had staked their claim as the nation's best college team. And it's no coincidence that their season ended in the Rose Bowl with a national title.

That Florida State team embraced pressure by adopting
the behaviors that led to a decisive win in Clemson. That
Clemson team shrank from the pressure. It's no accident
that two years later a Clemson team with great leaders
and great habits embraced the pressure and took back the
Atlantic Coast Conference from Florida State. The Tigers
built on that win and wound up playing for the national
title three times in four years, winning two. I'll bet they
had some meetings that looked an awful lot like the one we
had in Tallahassee in the summer of 2013.

What is pressure really? Pressure means you have ambition,
and that ambition can be in any area of your life. That
squeezing feeling of pressure is no different whether you
are Russell Wilson in the tunnel in Glendale, Arizona,
with "Bitter Sweet Symphony" playing and Tom Brady
across the field or you are a CFO preparing for an earnings
call with your board and stockholders listening or a
student preparing for a big exam or a parent helping your
child through a difficult moment in life. When we want
something, we will feel a pull toward it, but the best things
won't simply be given to us.

We don't experience pressure around the things that come
easily to us. But the things everyone wants but only a
select few can have? We feel that squeeze. Pressure can
be terrifying. Billie Jean King called it a privilege because
on the other side of it are truly incredible feelings and the
acquisition of something we value. The scariest places I've

found myself have been in the ocean when I'm swimming
far from shore. In those spots, my imagination can own me.
But I go immediately in my mind to the truth. Can I handle
this moment? I was born on a lake. I'm a strong swimmer.
But where's my fitness at? When is the last time I swam?
How is my tolerance for big waves? Pressure feels a lot like
swimming for me. Building a new business? Deep water
filled with waves. Separation? Divorce? Uncomfortable
waters. Rough. And incredibly cold. Pressure is best
navigated on two levels.

- Who am I now?

What have I done in my life to prepare myself to deal with
the pressure I face? This is a list of neutral statements that
help identify strengths and weaknesses. In the swimming
scenario, I made an honest evaluation of my swimming
ability. The divorce scenario is much more complicated, but
I still can evaluate the factors that can help me or harm me
going forward. On the plus side, I am still young enough to
find happiness with someone else. We didn't have children,
so we don't have to drag anyone else through this. I have
built a thriving business that allows me to be financially
secure and meet a diverse group of interesting, successful
people. On the negative side, I need to fix the issues that
harmed this marriage. I need to improve my work-life
balance.

- Who will I be?

Here we create our goal and make our plan to be ready
when pressure comes again. We take what we learned—
good and bad—from the last pressure situation and design
behaviors that should make us more successful the next
time around. If I barely make it back to shore in the
swimming scenario, I need to either practice swimming in
rough water more often or not swim so far from the shore.
In the divorce scenario, I need to thoroughly examine the
factors that led to the failure of the marriage and try to
build myself into a person who will be a better husband or
not get married again.

Want is a precursor to any success we have in our lives.
It's the starting point. Its inflection point is pressure. When
we want something there usually is a process that leads
to its attainment. Pressure becomes useful, especially at
an inflection point, because it puts us into a seeking mode
and we are open to the answers. Pressure also can be a
by-product of need. Ask anyone who has gotten laid off
unexpectedly about the pressure they felt. It's intense. I've
worked with multiple coaching staffs that got fired, and
that process is never easy. But the only way to get back on
your feet is to welcome that pressure. Running from it can
make a bad situation worse. By understanding that you've
reached an inflection point—even though it wasn't one
you chose—and by making a neutral assessment of your
situation that catalogs your abilities in relation to the job
market, you can overcome the shock and find what's next.
The pressure might make you reach out to people you were

scared to approach before. It might embolden you to try something you never would have before. It might lead you to a better situation if you steer into the pressure instead of away from it.

The key is to be ready when the pressure comes. When you're willing to jump over three chairs and grab the pen and take ownership, you're ready. Many of us live our lives like they're rental cars. We don't clean rental cars. We can ding them up without consequence. When we own a car, we tend to worry more about jumping curbs or scratching the rims. We wash the car. We wax it. We vacuum the floor mats. Your life isn't a rental car. You own it. And that means you must engage in the behaviors that keep it in good working order. If you do, it will respond when you press the gas when the driver of the semi in the next lane decides he wants to move into your lane but doesn't see you.

You need to be thinking neutrally, making plans, and making good choices so you're prepared when the pressure arrives. Someone is going to get what you want. It's up to you to make sure that person is you. You can behave your way into being ready even if you don't have the perfect God-given skill set for your situation. Someone else having a gift that you don't have isn't a valid excuse. Just ask Russell Wilson. Mike Glennon, the quarterback who sat behind Russell at NC State and took over when Russ transferred, was always viewed as the more naturally gifted quarterback. He had the height, the arm, the look. Which one of those guys won a Super Bowl, though? No outside force is going to bestow what we want on any of us. We have to follow the plan that we self-prescribe.

Are we for real? If I'm doing what I've intended to do in the manner it is supposed to be done, then I'm absolutely for fucking real. For the best at anything, the real pressure happens inside—not externally. But everyone is swimming in that dark ocean. Fear is real. Believe it. Still, we can all swim if we are willing to learn. And on the back side of accomplishment is a feeling that you can't buy. You can't snort it or take a pill for it. You earn it. Because you did it or you were a part of a team that did it. And when you live in those locker rooms you want more of it. Believe me. I've stood on the field in the Rose Bowl. The Superdome. The Orange Bowl. I didn't score a touchdown, but I felt like I had. That triumph and glory is what the back end of pressure feels like. And trust me, it's worth it.

It Takes Leadership

Nick Saban won a national title at LSU in 2003. After a two-year stint with the Miami Dolphins, he took the Alabama job in 2007 and won five more national titles in the next ten years. That's an astounding level of dominance that no one else has reached in this era of college football. How did Nick pull it off? He can do something almost no one else in his sport—or pretty much anywhere—can. He can convince a huge group of eighteen- to twenty-two-year-olds to perform consistently on a weekly basis. That age group doesn't usually do anything consistently, yet you always know what you're going to get from an Alabama team. The offensive linemen will block who they're supposed to block. The linebackers will fill the gaps they're supposed to fill. Crimson Tide players won't make an abundance of mental or physical mistakes. And they'll hit their opponents hard every play.

Nick has a more hard-nosed leadership style than most. He's supremely demanding. He isn't going to change his standards for individual players. But that doesn't mean he's unwilling to adapt. This willingness to adjust is a major reason his teams have remained so consistent.

For example, Nick realized as his career progressed that players were absorbing information differently than they had before. That's a big reason why he brought me aboard with the Miami Dolphins and at Alabama. He wanted another voice delivering the message in a different way. Often that voice was mine. Other times it belonged to someone whose story might resonate. One of my tasks at Alabama was to help choose guest speakers to address the team throughout the year. Nick wanted a diverse set of people speaking to the team because he'd discovered that while some players might adopt process-oriented, neutral thinking because Coach Saban preached about it every day, another player might need former Navy SEAL Marcus Luttrell delivering a similar message in order to truly understand. If Nick and his assistants talked about the illusion of choice and seventy-five players understood, the same message coming from Chris Herren, the basketball star who nearly lost everything because of drug addiction, might make that point sink in for five more players.

From the outside, Nick may seem old school and set in his ways, but those who have worked with him know he's one of the most inquisitive people in sports. He's always looking

for new ways to do everything and then stress-testing the
new practices against time-tested ones. After Alabama lost
to Ohio State in the Sugar Bowl following the 2014 season,
Nick invited Tom Herman to visit Alabama. Herman had
been the Ohio State offensive coordinator whose plays had
confounded Alabama's defense. Herman, who became
the head coach at Houston that off-season, accepted the
invitation thinking that he, as a first-time head coach, would
be picking the brain of Nick Saban. Instead, Nick peppered
Herman with questions about his offense. "How do you
do this?" "Why does this work so well?" Herman, who has
since become the head coach at Texas, realized during that
meeting why Nick has won so much. He may seem as if
he already knows everything, but he never stops trying to
adapt. Elements of Herman's offense appeared in Alabama's
offense the following season, and the Tide won another
national title.

Nick has been better than anyone at adapting his playbook
and personnel as the sport of football has changed, and
he also has stayed on the cutting edge of training players'
minds. By doing this, he gives them the tools to develop the
behaviors they can use to lead themselves when they don't
have a coach directing their every move.

Nick will tell you he wasn't born a great leader. He had
to hone his style. The process-oriented thinking—ignoring
the big picture and focusing on each successive detail to
reach a goal—wasn't something he taught when he was the

head coach at Toledo or the defensive coordinator with the Cleveland Browns. He began explaining it in earnest as the head coach at Michigan State in the 1990s. Lonny Rosen, a psychiatry professor at the school, had inspired Nick to think differently, and Nick began teaching that same method of thinking to his assistant coaches and his players. He honed that teaching more at LSU and with the Dolphins. By the time he got to Alabama, he had created an effective way to explain to players why they should worry not about the scoreboard but about the next snap. But he didn't set it in stone. Nick kept consulting Dr. Rosen, whose bushy beard inspires players to call him Gandalf. Nick hired me and kept me around for eight years.

Nick also has worked for most of his career to overcome personality traits that might hinder his effectiveness as a leader. For example, he is an introvert who turned himself into an exceptional communicator. Why? Because you have to communicate to lead. He values being effective more than being comfortable. He values being heard. He wasn't gifted that way. He made himself that way so he could lead more effectively.

This is not a book specifically about leadership. But anyone who chooses a path toward greatness is going to have to stare this concept down and see where they stand in relation to it. Even if you aren't a manager, you have to lead yourself. (And if you lead yourself well, you may get promoted and wind up leading others.) If you're a parent, you have to lead your children. Everyone needs to know how to lead, and everyone needs to know how to recognize effective and ineffective leaders and understand why those people succeed or fail.

We've discussed competency for athletes and performers, but we can break it down the same way for leaders and those who coach others, regardless of industry.

Unconscious Incompetence

Tough to play for. Tougher to work for. Toughest to live with. Loss or adversity is typically the best teacher for those in this state. Clear, objective data works as well. I don't spend time around these people often because they don't hire me. They don't know what they don't know, so they'd never admit to themselves that they needed help reaching their players. Even if they did, I'd probably struggle to help them because they tend to be extremely closed-minded to any ideas that didn't come from their formative years in the profession.

I have had opportunities to observe these types, however. When Nick Saban left the Miami Dolphins, I was asked to come in and meet with the new leadership group. This surprised me, but Kevin O'Neill, the longtime trainer who worked under Jimmy Johnson, Dave Wannstedt, and Saban, saw a value in the players continuing to have access to me even though Nick had moved on. As I entered the room, it was friendly. The team's salary cap guy and attorney were with Kevin, and I updated them on my upcoming wedding, which was a few days away in Sarasota. Moments later the new coach walked into the room. His opening statement? "Who the fuck are we meeting with today?" Followed by "Did Saban also have this asshole on a ten-year contract?" I wasn't even going to get my four minutes. Kevin did a great job of framing who I was and why he thought the meeting was important. He also mentioned that I was no longer under contract. In five minutes, I knew this guy was going to get his ass kicked as a head coach. Not because he was a dickhead. Many head coaches and CEOs share that trait. Not because he was an asshole to me. I've dealt with my share of that over the years. I knew it because he clearly didn't respect Kevin O'Neill's institutional memory. Kevin was talented and he was capable and he had been around the league for a long time. That doesn't happen by accident. If he felt a meeting was important, then a future winner would value that perspective.

For the first sixty minutes the new coach motherfucked me because I hadn't played in the NFL and he didn't think I'd earned the relevance I'd had the season before under Coach Saban. I listened. Kevin did as well. We both knew that you can't confront people who don't know they don't know. I waited patiently to see if he actually had any interest in utilizing someone like me. I understood the reality that this wasn't personal, even though it could easily be received that way.

This guy was grandiose as fuck. He wasn't willing to allow other perspectives to stand alongside his own. He thought he'd win because of his genius. He didn't realize winning is a collaborative effort that requires leaders who are willing to listen to people who have valuable perspectives. (Not me in this case, but Kevin, who knew exactly how the organization functioned.) More important than believing in yourself is believing in what you are doing for yourself and those you are serving. And the leader is supposed to serve the subordinates. Part of that service is a willingness to listen and learn. I don't think he understood that. He went 1–15. There are no accidents.

Conscious Incompetence

These leaders have learned that they have some roadblocks. This may have happened by losing a job, barely holding on to it, losing employees, public exposure, or personal discovery. This doesn't mean they have any interest in addressing these issues, but they do know they exist. Think of it this way: the reason we visit doctors is to get a clear diagnosis. That's important. But the treatment is optional. We can opt in or out. Too many people say, "I am what I am." That is a statement of surrender. It means you aren't willing to learn and grow and adapt as the environment changes. Even worse, you know you aren't willing to change.

You are what you do, and you've become what you've done. But who you can and will become lies in who you are next, and that will be determined by what you do next and how you address the roadblocks on the immediate road you're traveling. Too many organizations and their leaders are consciously incompetent. People know the problems, but don't act to change them. I've sat in so many rooms where everyone knew. Everyone. CEOs. Commanding officers. Entertainment figures. Sports business icons. And they didn't address the problems. They said they were what they were, and that was that.

This might be the most unforgivable leadership state, because problems get identified but never get solved because the leader is unwilling to try. If this describes your boss, you may want to seek a new environment. If you *are* the boss and you're wondering if this describes you, don't worry. You wouldn't have bought this book in the first place if it did. You'd have said "I am who I am" and kept on moving.

Unconscious Competence

We know these people very well in music and sports.

In 1982, English bandleader Kevin Rowland co-wrote a song about one of his teenage relationships. In the video were violins, a banjo, and a whole lot of overalls. A nascent MTV, still starved for content, played that video constantly. Everyone loved the violins, the banjo, and the overalls, and "Come On Eileen" became a massive hit for Dexy's Midnight Runners. It hit number one on the Billboard Hot 100 and for a moment in time was the biggest song in the world.

By 1987, Dexy's had broken up. Nothing else the band recorded had anywhere near the impact of "Eileen." The lineup had shifted because of personality conflicts. The looks changed. The sound changed. Rowland never could reproduce that magic.

Florida State football wasn't the same after Telvin Smith left. As hard as it is to say, much of the success of the 2013 national championship was the magic of the team's personnel. Leaders shine like this for windows of time. They have moments when they are everything they need to be. They succeed. Then they fail. They get divorced. Face a miscarriage. Lose employees. And their understanding of how they succeeded isn't strong enough to deal with the shit life is going to bring their way. They knew, but they didn't know why they knew. We see this a lot in college football because the players are on the team only for the time they're in college. With so much roster turnover, leaders are difficult enough to replace. And leaders who are unconsciously competent can't teach the next group how to replicate their leadership style.

So when the new leaders on a team need to know again—to really know—they don't have the substance to find those answers. They don't have the foundation, people, resources, preparation, legwork, or adversity tolerance to execute what drives their success independent of circumstances. The upside of unconsciously competent leaders is very clear. You know it's in them. They know it too. To win and succeed in your organization, to become a team of legacy, you've got to get this population to discover why what they've done has worked. Those leaders need to learn how they helped their teams succeed and how to replicate that leadership when the circumstances change. To achieve that, those leaders need to do some neutral thinking. They need to create an unbiased analysis of their successes and failures. They need to list the behaviors that worked and the ones that didn't. If they are honest in their analysis, there is a great chance they'll join this next group.

Conscious Competence

A restaurant becomes exceptional not only for the level of its food but for the fact that it can reach that level consistently. Alain Ducasse is one of the best chefs of our time. He's one of two to hold twenty-one Michelin stars. His attention for detail is epic, and he's been able to scale his businesses across the globe for a very clear reason. He knows why he's good, and he knows how to implement his process.

Olympic swimmer Michael Phelps's level of success is so
great that if he were a competing nation, he'd rank thirty-
ninth in all-time medal count. Phelps's "leader" is coach Bob
Bowman. Bowman's attention to detail is available to other
swimmers as well as other coaches. Most won't copy it. And
it doesn't work for every swimmer. But it was perfect for
Phelps. In an essay he wrote for the American Swimming
Coaches Association, Bowman explained working with a
preteen Phelps. Bowman was trying to fix Phelps's freestyle
technique, and he noticed that Phelps swam his best times
when he used a six-beat kick, which means the swimmer
is kicking six times per stroke cycle. Bowman tried simply
suggesting the six-beat kick and he tried praising Phelps
when he used the correct kick, but neither strategy inspired
Phelps to use the six-beat kick consistently. Bowman had
noticed that what Phelps hated more than anything was
getting thrown out of practice. Dismissing him to the
lobby of the pool almost always produced a more focused
swimmer at the next workout. So Bowman told the young
Phelps that he would throw him out of practice every time
he saw Phelps use a two-beat kick instead of a six-beat.
The first day, Phelps made it 400 yards before he used a
two-beat and got tossed out of practice. The second day, he
made it 800. By the end of the week, he made it 6,000. The
following week he was using only six beats. Not all coaches
would resort to this, but Bowman had examined Phelps's
learning style and found the most effective motivational
technique. He had been willing to try different methods
and kept tweaking until he found the one that produced the

best result. That is consciously competent leadership, and that's what you should strive to be when leading yourself or others.

I open up many meetings with an educational video called *Why Winners Win.* It features stars from all walks of life discussing why they're successful, and it includes plenty of examples of great leaders.

LeBron James talking to his Cleveland Cavalier teammates before the NBA finals: "We went through every task. We went through everything. Everything—odds against us. But we're here. Let's get through it, all right? By any means necessary. You pick your brother up if he's down. At all times, you cover for one another. Hold your end of the bargain up, all right? Don't rely on nobody, but know that you've got help."[1]

Volleyball star Kerri Walsh Jennings discussing her relationship with playing partner Misty May-Treanor: "Bottom line, if you have respect in your partnership, in your team, in whatever you're doing, people are going to step up and lead. People are going to fall back. But you have the same mission, and that's where the success comes from."

Apple CEO Tim Cook discussing what he learned from predecessor Steve Jobs: "In every way, at every turn, the question we ask ourselves is not 'What can we do?' but 'What should we do?' Because Steve taught us that's how change happens. And from him I learned to never be content with the way that things are."[2]

Alibaba cofounder Joseph Tsai discussing what matters in his company's culture: "It's the values of teamwork. It's the values of discipline. And, very important, the value of preparation."[3]

Former UK prime minister Tony Blair: "People often ask me about leadership, and I say leadership is about wanting the responsibility to be on your shoulders. Not ignoring its weight, but knowing someone has to carry it and reaching out for that person to be you. Leaders are heat seekers, not heat deflectors."[4]

You don't have to be born a heat seeker. Anyone can become this. Start by studying your own successes. We learn best from those. Then understand your barriers.

Two mistruths hamper too many would-be leaders today:

I'm introverted, so I can't lead groups or communicate well.

Nick Saban is introverted. He didn't say that. Instead of offering that excuse, which would have been an example of conscious incompetence, he chose instead to work to become a better communicator.

I'm extroverted, so I can't listen to people individually very well.

Every consciously competent leader listens to the people above, below, and alongside them. Listening allows those leaders first to become conscious of what needs improvement. Then it allows those leaders to build competence in those areas.

Listening and studying successes and failures won't help you only if you're in charge of other people. It can also help you as a subordinate as you try to navigate your relationships with the people in charge of you.

If no one can impact you like you can impact you—which is what this whole book is about—then while I acknowledge that fucked-up coaches or CEOs or supervisors can take an organization down a dark path, it also needs to be said that players and employees alike can recognize those leaders for what they are: fucked up. And many great teams overcome shitty leadership on a consistent daily basis because they adapt and find ways to push through it. Why? Because it takes what it takes. The way they express this in the Navy SEAL community is "find an excuse to win." Simply put, you must overcome your circumstances. Even if those circumstances include a shitty boss.

So if you say "If only I worked there" or "If only she were my supervisor" or "If only my team had more organization" or "This book said we need this to succeed," you'd be wrong. Do not excuse yourself to yourself. Wherever you are, right now, today, there is a path to manage your situation without replacing the people around you. I've seen that. I've lived that. Teams win that way all the time. This hinges largely on you addressing you by developing the skills we've been discussing since you cracked open this book. You can also help yourself by understanding why leaders sometimes interact differently with different employees.

If you're a talented employee with a boss constantly applying pressure, there's probably a reason for that. Head coaches or high-performing captains in the sports and military worlds are often grinders. Things didn't come easily to them. They had to work to master their crafts. (Conversely, there is a reason supremely talented athletes rarely become great coaches. Those people have some gifts that can't be taught, and they don't always understand why their players can't learn those talents.) Because of this, the grinder coaches sometimes develop an almost primal aversion to gifted performers who don't fulfill their gifts.

This can work positively or negatively for the leader. If that feeling makes the leader work to find ways to push the underperforming gifted person to a better performance, that's great for everyone in the organization. But sometimes the result is a feeling of bitterness from someone who didn't have those talents and can't empathize or understand why someone who is gifted wouldn't seek to maximize their gifts. This can blind leaders and cause them to make some stupid decisions. I've seen it. The American soccer

world was filled with leaders like that. Many athletes and
employees simply don't have the aptitude their peers do.
Gifted performers operating at 60 percent are better than
their "try-hard" peers at 100 percent. Why am I saying this?
Because I am a try-hard peer. If someone's 70 percent is
better than another's 100 percent, you have a responsibility
to recognize that and play the person who will produce
better results—regardless of if you want to punish that
person for not taking full advantage of the gifts you wish
you had. You also have a responsibility to try to help that
person maximize those gifts, but not through punishments
that harm the entire organization.

The best leaders manage underachieving talent at an elite
level. They challenge those employees. They show them the
bigger opportunity. They monitor behavior and guide it as
well as they can, but they accept the reality that being good
gets in the way of being great all the time. When good is
actually good enough in specific areas of a program, team,
or organization, you accept that. And good is still better
than the best effort that yields only average.

I learned this lesson while working with soccer player
Freddy Adu, who may go down as one of the most
unrealized talents in American sports history. When
developing young talent an organization needs to lead with
both confidence and an incredible amount of humility. The
American soccer brain trust—US Soccer and Major League
Soccer—didn't use much of either during the transition of

Freddy from global youth phenom to professional athlete.
Freddy began his life in Ghana, but moved to Rockville,
Maryland, at age eight when his mother won a green
card lottery. Not long after he arrived in America, he was
identified as a prodigy. In 2004, he was the number one
pick in the MLS draft. He was fourteen, and he was *that*
good.

Freddy's fellow phenoms at the time were LeBron James,
who entered the NBA in 2003 as an eighteen-year-old, and
golfer Michelle Wie, who turned professional just before her
sixteenth birthday in 2005. Wie has had a solid but injury-
riddled career. She won the US Women's Open in 2014 and
has won four other LPGA tournaments. LeBron is one of the
best players in the history of his sport. Freddy? He played
for fourteen teams in fourteen years and at thirty found
himself muddling through in a second-tier American league.

That's a long way from the next Pelé, which was what
everyone expected of young Freddy. Reputations like this
aren't given. They are earned. I watched Freddy earn his
while training with US Soccer's developmental teams
at IMG Academy, which is how I came to work with
him. Freddy had succeeded and lived up to the hype at
every turn leading up to his MLS debut in 2004. When
the US played Brazil at the under-17 or under-20 World
Cup tournaments, the Brazilians were lining up—fighting
even—to get Freddy's jersey when the teams traded them
after games. The true proof of his unique skill set flashed

in his first under-20 World Cup in 2003. He was fourteen, competing against the very best nineteen-year-olds in the world. He had gotten a late call to play for Coach Thomas Rongen's team. That group featured future US men's national team stars Clint Dempsey, Eddie Johnson, Bobby Convey, and many others who already had been tested in European pro leagues or in MLS. Rongen wouldn't give Freddy any favor, but he also didn't create any unnecessary roadblocks that would show a lack of favoritism. If Freddy was good enough, he'd play. By the second game in the tournament in Dubai, Freddy had earned a starting spot. He showed why in a quarterfinal loss to powerhouse Argentina when he raced seventy yards before flicking a pass to set up a Convey goal. I watched this game in Bradenton with USMNT player Tony Sanneh. After that play, he turned to me and said, "Wow. This kid is for real. You aren't doing that at a U-20 event if you don't have elite ability."

Freddy's upward trajectory would stall, though. His transition to professional soccer proved treacherous. While the Cleveland Cavaliers nurtured LeBron, DC United never quite seemed to know how to handle its young star.

Great leadership requires an ability to develop strong followership. Those being led have to have a general understanding of who and what they're following. Credibility matters. Major League Soccer held a fourteen-year-old Freddy Adu up as a player who would revolutionize soccer in this country. The league's ability to keep him in America as opposed to him leaving for a top league in England or Italy was touted as a significant victory for US Soccer.

What happened was the equivalent of Alex Rodriguez being sent to France at age fifteen to develop as a baseball talent. Had that happened, A-Rod would have had to overcome the fact that France didn't have a clue how to develop world-class talent in that sport. The same goes for the US and soccer. The people I'd meet both in MLS and at US Soccer would stun me with their lack of humility. I'd come back to Bradenton after working with the Miami Dolphins or Jacksonville Jaguars and interact with top leaders from MLS or US Soccer who were visiting the academy. On any subject—but particularly when the subject was Freddy—there was no humility. No inquisitiveness. No acknowledgment of the inevitable risks associated with trying to develop a young talent in a place not known for developing young talents.

I was at dinner with Earnie Stewart, a USMNT and European pro soccer veteran who would later be a teammate of Freddy's, and I told Earnie how concerned I was about the entire process. Earnie actually thanked me for saying that, because he knew how challenging this journey would be. Earnie now runs US Soccer, and I believe his experience makes him more battle tested and gives him a broader perspective like his counterparts who run the NBA, NFL, and Major League Baseball. Unfortunately,

Earnie wasn't in charge when Freddy was in his formative years.

I've always believed that there are certain athletes who are "environmental" performers. This means that if their gifts and talents are managed in concert with the right structure— where they simply do what is required daily and don't have the ability or the opportunity to make bad choices—they will succeed. This was Freddy. John Ellinger, the IMG Performance Institute, the US U-17 coaching staff, Freddy's U-17 teammates, Chad Bohling, myself, and a number of visiting world-class athletes in Bradenton helped steer Freddy at a young age to see how world-class behavior leads to world-class performance. It was a marketing campaign from the outside in. We hit Freddy with the same kind of restrictions and routines that had made tennis star Andre Agassi both love and hate Bradenton. We didn't leave Freddy anything to do but train, and that was the best ally for his gifts. Sleep? Proper diet? Stretching? Practice? Those things weren't optional. When Freddy was in Bradenton, I'd get calls every weekend from Gary Cohen, the supervisor of the academy's students, because Freddy would get caught jumping the fence to play soccer on the external fields. That's the worst thing he did there: jumped the fence to play more soccer. He lived it. He loved it. He dominated the sport.

I pulled Freddy into many meetings with Eli Manning, Michael Johnson, Clint Mathis, and Anquan Boldin. I brought him in to eat with them and get additional mentoring. I knew his life would resemble theirs more than those of many traditional or current American soccer players, and I wanted him to understand their processes. Looking back, however, I see now that this created a sense of entitlement in Freddy and a bull's-eye on his back in the eyes of the other players due to what they considered special treatment. In addition, Freddy was thirteen. He was mature. Bright. A true savant. But as he aged he struggled to embrace the grind that's not optional with the management of such incredible gifts. Pro sports would not provide the structure that the academy would. His first coach in MLS would not be Paul Silas, whom the Cavaliers had installed to help LeBron navigate his early years in the NBA. Piotr Nowak at DC United had been a good player, but he had never coached before he took over the team Freddy's rookie season. I believe his decision not to start Freddy in his first game—despite MLS hyping Freddy that entire off-season— was the beginning of the end of Freddy's career. Trying to prove Freddy wasn't getting preferential treatment backfired, and Freddy spiraled. A series of mistakes made by Freddy, myself, and a lot of other people operating on a trial-and-error basis turned the phenom into a cautionary tale.

A-Rod didn't develop in France. He was a product of Major League Baseball. The league had operated for ninety-one years before he set foot in it. Freddy entered an eight-year-old league with no record for developing top talent. That was a risk that should never have been allowed. He didn't have the discipline or behaviors to overcome that decision.

We live and we learn. When Freddy left Bradenton to begin his journey into professional sports, many of the behaviors that had fueled his success didn't make the trip with him to DC. Maybe he would have learned that had he gone to a club in Europe. Maybe they would have had more experience with that kind of talent and might have known how to focus it better. That still keeps me up at night. It will remain one of the biggest failures in my career and a burden I'll forever share with Freddy Adu.

I still believe that had we handled Freddy properly, we might have been able to help him come closer to maximizing his talents. Would his coaches have had to spend more time on him than on the other players? Absolutely. But it would have been worth it.

Always Bet on Talent

The Pareto principle is also known as the 80/20 rule, or the idea that 80 percent of the effects come from 20 percent of the causes. That means most issues and most successes come from a relatively small group of people, and how those people get managed will determine the success or failure of the organization.

A leader's job—whether CEO, middle manager, high school principal, or coach—is managing the ratio of actively

disengaged employees to actively engaged employees.
Based on the great teams I've worked with, I believe these
percentages to be as accurate in the sports world as they
are in the business world. This stuns people who haven't
spent time in high-performing organizations or teams.
The reality is we win with strong pluralities. We need the
right force multipliers. We need to know how to minimize
a capable talent's relevance when they're actively
disengaged, but more important, we need to hold people
accountable to the talent, aptitude, skill, and gifts they
have. Nick Saban reminded good players that they "were
supposed to play good." Your organization doesn't win
by fixing all the problem employees. Your organization
wins when the best and the baddest live up to the promise
they've led you to believe they have. They need to do it
consistently.

Betting on talent is still always the correct calculation. As
much as the person may drive you fucking crazy, don't
downplay their gifts. They matter. And understand that, in
many cases, if they didn't have talent they would try a lot
fucking harder. That's the paradox. So educate them. Help
them. *Lead them.* I always wished some soccer version of
Jimbo or Nick Saban or Nick Bollettieri or Duke basketball
coach Mike Krzyzewski had gotten Freddy when he
was young. They wouldn't have judged his peculiarities.
They'd have helped him see the opportunity in front of
him by aggregating the correct behaviors. Instead, he was
typically scolded for what he didn't do and affirmed as lazy,

uncommitted, and a waste of talent, and he lived down to that. This happens all too often in every field.

We didn't lead Freddy correctly. All of us could learn from our mistakes. Like anything else, leadership is a set of behaviors. It's not destiny. It can be trained. It can be improved.

The ability to influence the behavior of others through leadership moves a team from being a collection of players to becoming an established program. What's the difference? A team has a one-year shelf life. Period. When he worked at Florida State, Jimbo Fisher would remind players of that all the time. A team's component parts reshuffle every year, and the record reflects the sum of its parts and behaviors in that window of time. As the players move on, many of them will take those behaviors, gifts, and skill sets with them. And that can be brutal if you're the coach tasked with replacing skilled players with excellent behaviors. A program is a collection of behaviors that translates forward. This happens through a well-developed process, continuing education, and a clear set of choices that the coaches and players know are required regardless of the names on the backs of the jerseys. This was what I saw Alabama become. Florida State had a similar but shorter run at this. Georgia's football program, which I began working with in 2016, is becoming this right now.

There is a very clear formula for managing others, but it isn't that different from the formula I've set out in this book for managing ourselves. That's why if you master these principles, you should be able to lead yourself and others equally well. Success for leaders is in the simplicity. Seek the clues left by great leaders. Adopt them. Adapt when needed. The world needs less ignorance. We need fewer followers.

11

It Takes Role Models

Attitude is contagious. The right attitudes can be particularly contagious. The best teams, organizations, units, and even countries are led by people who have this ability to influence. To inspire. These are people we can't help but want to emulate.

I've built much of my educational platform on the power of this premise. Why role models matter is clear. They are living, behaving, operating in the real world in ways we hope to. Derek Jeter mattered to Russell Wilson. Russell saw behavior, character, and abilities in Jeter that he believed he could attain. So he studied. He learned. He emulated. In that journey, he became better. There is only one Derek Jeter. But Jeter's behaviors aren't copyrighted. Anyone can copy them. They were available to Russ and they are available to anyone else who wants to emulate a

person who consistently makes the correct choices. Role
models matter.

The most powerful role models aren't usually the ones
we watch in stadiums full of screaming fans. They aren't
movie stars. They aren't CEOs. They are people we see
every day. Russell wanted to be like Derek Jeter, but the
man he most wanted to emulate was his dad, Harrison
Wilson III. Harry B., as he was known to his football and
baseball teammates, was a two-sport star at Dartmouth
who went on to earn a law degree from Virginia. He was a
successful attorney who raised three successful children—
Harrison IV, Russell, and Anna—prior to his death from
diabetes complications in 2010. Russell has spent his entire
life trying to follow his dad's example.

I don't have much in common with a Super Bowl–winning
quarterback, but Russell and I do share one trait: our dads
were our heroes.

My dad was an original.

In the 1960s and '70s, Bob Moawad navigated a successful
high school coaching and teaching career. He even won
a state basketball title. After twelve years in education
he would feel a pull to keep teaching—but not in the
traditional sense. He wanted to work more fundamentally
than he was able to do in the classroom; he wanted to
work in and around the human mind and to help people

build their belief systems. His move into the motivational field coincided with my birth. That's how I became a living case study for him. As I grew up, I watched him build a business called Edge Learning Institute. I watched schools and businesses adopt his Increasing Human Effectiveness program. He traveled the country—and became a celebrity of sorts in the Pacific Northwest—lecturing at schools and companies. He taught people that their attitudes could influence their outcomes. He even served for a time as the president of the National Association for Self Esteem. Little did I know that years later I'd feel that same calling. I'd leave classroom teaching and enter a field that—crazy as it seems—hadn't changed much in twenty-five years.

My dad had a magnetic personality. He was authentic. He was confident. I never questioned that he both lived and believed everything he taught. And in 1999—after being told at fifty-nine that he had less than one year to live—I saw him attack his plan, create his own personal ad campaign, eliminate the controllable negatives, master his own language, and behave in alignment with both the choices and mentality that would give someone a fighting chance against multiple myeloma. And he lived until 2007.

He lived what he taught. If he was walking off the golf course, people would say things like "Saw your score, Bob. I guess that positivity didn't get you over the top today." Or "Mr. Positive! How we doing today?!"

What stood out was how confidently he took that in stride, no matter how condescending the message. When people would press him he'd simply say, "You're right, and I can't prove that positive thinking works all the time. My score on the back nine may indicate that, but I do know that negative thinking does work. It works negatively 100 percent of the time."

It felt as if my dad were perpetually playing defense. For some reason, the idea of trying to boost the self-esteem of young people made some older people angry, and my dad found himself explaining the movement frequently. He was even asked to defend the momentum that was growing for self-esteem education in public high schools to John Stossel during a segment of ABC's *20/20*.

You remember *20/20*, right? It came on at 10:00 on Friday nights. There would be a story about the solving of a cold-case murder or a Barbara Walters interview with a celebrity, and every so often they'd throw in a piece where Stossel would examine a new trend. Stossel would challenge whatever idea he examined, asking really tough questions. It made for good TV, except when your dad was in the crosshairs. In 1998, my dad went head-to-head with Stossel on *20/20*. My dad believed that self-esteem didn't necessarily need to come from achievement. It could be encouraged and fostered. It could come from within. My dad believed that he could encourage a non-reader to be a better reader by telling him he was a good reader. John

Stossel challenged him, accused him of "lying" to children. He also called my dad a "nut." But my dad held his ground, admirably, authoritatively, calmly. And insisted in the power of affirming of what we are capable of becoming.

Stossel went on to suggest that school shootings might be a result of the crash of someone with artificially inflated self-esteem. It was infuriating, to watch my dad be put on the defensive about something that I knew could help people, but he handled all these situations with calm and class. Just like with the guys on the golf course, he'd explain that while he didn't have definitive evidence positive thinking worked, he knew negative thinking worked negatively every single time.

People ask me all the time how I wound up preaching neutral thinking after hearing my dad preach about self-esteem for my entire life. It's actually pretty easy.

Negative or positive were the options I was given as a child. These are the options you've probably been given your entire life. Most of us define every thought that passes through our minds by placing it on one of these two poles.

I grew up in a home where my father's full-time job focused on helping people choose—to the degree they could— between negative and positive. IBM. NASA. The governor of Washington. School districts. The ROTC. Cancer patients. These were just some of the many who leaned on him for

critical support. I, of course, leaned on him too. He was
my dad, and whether I knew it or not as a kid, he was my
hero. Bob Moawad spent thirty-three of his sixty-five years
on Earth fighting to see the best in everything both for and
with thousands of people. He was blazing a trail in a field
that had existed for less than thirty years when he entered
it. All he had were negative and positive, and he was
working so hard to fight negativity that it didn't occur to
him to consider that there might be another possibility.

But for me? His youngest son, his science project, his test
case, I would need more. Negative and positive weren't
enough. I wouldn't fully grasp this until I got deeper into
my own life's journey. Even when I didn't have a name for
it, I recognized that there was a way of thinking that could
save us from negative and give us more than positive. When
I heard Michael Johnson explain his success to NFL draft
prospects. When I watched Nick Bollettieri coach Serena
Williams. When I met Nick Saban and learned how he
approaches every practice. And whether he knew it or not, I
also learned neutral from my dad. Not because it's what he
preached, but because it's the way he lived. Every day, I'm
trying to follow his example with my own behaviors.

The best role models, like my dad or Russell's dad, can
make other people believe more deeply in themselves. In the
mission. In the process. In the vision. The people I aspire
to emulate have helped me help myself and, as simple and
primal as it sounds, they have helped me ultimately feel

better about me. People like Nick Bollettieri, who will still call just to see how I'm doing. Or people like Russell, who sends handwritten notes to say thank you after a season. Or people like Jimbo Fisher, who answered his phone and helped me through one of my life's toughest moments.

As a young teacher in the LA Unified School District, I learned this lesson on the deepest level. On my last day as a teacher in Los Angeles, I received a three-foot-by-five-foot letter from a student. He hadn't been in any of my classes. In fact, I had to think deeply to remember our interactions. But over the two years I'd been at his school, I had said hello to him in the halls every time I saw him. I recognized he had a hunchback, and I knew how tough a physiological difference can be in high school. We sat down and ate together four or five times over the years, and he always had a smile for me and a "Hi, Mr. Moa!" I always tried to return it. As his graduation approached and the school year ended, I was excited to move on from LA. It was a tough place to teach, and I wasn't sure I was making the difference I'd hoped to. I'd committed to teaching at a private school in Florida with smaller class sizes and more resources. What I'd learn opening the letter was something you'll hear Nick Saban, Jimbo Fisher, and Kirby Smart say often: *Who you are speaks so loudly I can't hear a word you say.*

The letter was simple. "Mr. Moa—thank you for saying hello to me these last two years. You have no idea how much it meant to me."

I was stunned. I realized I *was* a role model. Maybe not a mentor to every student, but I had set an example by the way I lived and approached each day. I think the illusion is thinking we can choose not to carry this weight. I carried it at twenty-one whether I believed it or not. A role model is a heat seeker, not a heat deflector. We all need to be aware of this responsibility. Because you never know who is paying attention, and your actions may be providing an example— good or bad—for someone else.

My father didn't spend every waking moment trying to mentor me. But he was always teaching me. I learned what I needed to become by watching the way he lived. I can't think of anything more powerful.

12

It Takes What It Takes

I flew back to Washington from Florida for two days in 2006 for the baptism of the daughter of one of my closest friends. At the time, my father was fighting cancer as only he could. I walked into our guest room at the family home to see him reviewing a series of first-person affirmations exactly the way he had taught me to do beginning at age four.

I was no sicker the day of diagnosis than I was the day before.

I am living with—not dying of—cancer.

Hope and hopelessness are both choices. I've chosen hope.

I will not allow others to steal my hope or extinguish my pilot light.

I watched him for what felt like hours. I was in awe. He had already outlived his prognosis by five years at this point, but the high points had diminished and the grind was continuous. I finally spoke.

Me: *Hi, Dad.*

Dad: *Hi, son.*

Me: *It's all real, isn't it?*

Dad: *What's that, son?*

Me: *What you teach. The language. The statements. The programming. The ad campaign. All of it. Here you are, Dad. Battling* this. *Doing everything you told me to do as a college basketball player to succeed.*

Dad: *It is. Remember—when going through any difficulty— your alternatives.*

He seemed to gain strength as he said this.

Me: *What alternatives?*

Dad: *Choice. That's it. It's really the last true freedom any of us always have.*

Me: *Choosing what? Your response in this situation? I mean, I'm scared, Dad. I might be 2,000 miles away, I might seem tough, but I think about what you and Mom are having to handle every day.*

Dad: *Fear and worry can be involuntary. I fight that too. It's okay. But choice is not involuntary. You can take fear and worry out of your mind by not feeding it, and then what? Well, you've put yourself in a powerful position. Understand?*

Me: *I do.*

Dad: *I've never denied the diagnosis I face. You shouldn't either. I challenge the verdict, and I choose my language. I choose what I put into my mind. I choose how I manage the truth of this situation, and I just keep fighting. Working. Living. Everything I've ever told you your whole life, and millions of people, I'm counting on now.*

I remember that moment like it happened this morning. It would be one of our final conversations in person. Looking back now, it's amazing to see how my dad—who wouldn't live long enough to see me teach neutral thinking—naturally reverted to neutral thought as he fought for his life.

Thinking about the way my dad handled his final days makes me sure the lessons you've learned in this book work. Not because they're effective in the sports world. Not because they're effective in the business world. But because when the strongest, smartest people face the toughest challenges of their lives, their instinct is to think neutrally.

I've had the honor of working alongside US Navy SEAL Marcus Luttrell over the years. He told his story in *Lone*

Survivor, and it's a testament to staying neutral. In June 2005, Marcus and three other members of SEAL Team Ten were dispatched into the Hindu Kush mountains in eastern Afghanistan with a mission to either kill or capture a Taliban leader. After a group of goat herders stumbled upon the SEALs and gave their location to Taliban soldiers, the Taliban attacked. Luttrell's three teammates were killed and he was left to try to survive an enemy onslaught in an unfamiliar area. Luttrell was shot eleven times. He broke his back and his pelvis and blew out his knees. He broke his nose and bit off a piece of his tongue.

He needed to travel seven miles to reach the nearest village to have any chance of survival. But he didn't think about the total distance he had to cover. That would have overwhelmed him and made him quit. As he lay on the ground looking at the moon, he decided to crawl.

He grabbed a rock and drew a line in the dirt. Then he crawled forward. When his feet passed the line, he drew another line. He did that for seven miles. That is the ultimate in neutral thinking.

Marcus didn't think positively. He didn't think negatively. He thought, "I am capable of crawling to this line."

The next time life presents you with a challenge, don't simply assume everything will work out. Don't tell yourself you can't do it. Just evaluate the situation. Figure out what you can accomplish right now. Then draw your line. When you cross that line, draw another one. And keep going.

There will be times when all you have is yourself. After my marriage collapsed, there were moments when I tried to lean on people, and they weren't there. They were living *their* lives. This helped me remember to stop leaning and stand the fuck up.

I had to remember to manage my language. To watch what I consumed. To get to neutral. I had to repeatedly identify and live the behaviors I know have helped me and others. To look to my own successes for the strongest clues. Once I did, I could ask myself the most fundamental and powerful question:

What is it that I want?

Atherosclerosis is a hardening of the arteries. Psychosclerosis is a hardening of the attitudes, and it might be just as dangerous. No one does this *to* us. Life doesn't wear us down. We do it to ourselves. But there is a cure. It's inside all of us. That cure is the comma. The late comedian Gracie Allen said to never place a period where God has placed a comma. The idea of living neutral is putting a comma at the end of an event—good or bad—and knowing that the next words will determine how the sentence continues. I have the most powerful chance to keep writing my sentence for myself. If I don't, someone else will write it and I'll be forced to live it.

In 1975, a man named Lawrence Hildonen appeared in a Portland, Oregon, courtroom and begged the judge to send him back to jail. Hildonen had spent twenty-two of his forty-five years imprisoned. According to a story that appeared in Tacoma's *News Tribune*, Hildonen had been released after doing a stint for forgery. He found the ensuing eight weeks of freedom "terrifying," so he tried to rob a bank and waited to be arrested. He then asked the judge to dispense with the formalities and put him back behind bars. "I want to go home," Hildonen told the judge.[1]

Isn't it amazing what can become "home" to us? What's home to you right now? In your health? Your relationships? Your work life? Your family life? What are you willing to accept?

I've been blessed to serve a population of elite athletes. Most of them choose not to compromise. Most of them never have been and never will be complacent. They always want more. They always want to get better. That's such a powerful starting point. Wanting leads to questions. Those questions make us look at the role choice plays in our life relative to the things we want. That pushes us to make a plan. From there the barriers become clear, and the solutions quickly follow. When our mind sees solutions, we begin to adopt the best behaviors. We can approach life neutrally and do what we must do to produce the outcomes we desire. Once we reach this point, we know.

It takes what it takes.

Acknowledgments

My father challenged me to think bigger and deeper from a young age. "A mind once shaped by a new thought," he'd say, "will never go back to its previous version." But life has a way of narrowing that psychological growth for all of us.

I want to thank Maria Shriver for asking me to see a world larger than the sports fields or pristine Southern stadiums run by the top coaches and athletes. I will never forget sitting in her office in Brentwood, California, with Sandy Gleysteen, wondering to myself just why I was asked there. Little did I know, that meeting began a course correction that would change my life forever. It was Maria who believed my voice was meant for more; only time will tell if that's true, but I would never have attempted to take this step had she not asked me to speak to a larger audience, and maybe even for a deeper purpose.

Andy Staples, I can't thank you enough for your willingness to jump in headfirst with me. I've read your cover stories for years in *Sports Illustrated* and I'm excited to continue reading them on *The Athletic*. You are exceptional and knew exactly how to get us through this together. Thank you for saying yes, and most importantly, thanks to your family who allowed you to take this challenge head-on amidst your many other responsibilities.

Shannon Welch, you are the most polite and coolest version of an SEC head football coach I've ever met. The simple truth is you have all their grit, toughness, and ability to cut through the bullshit. Thank you for your neutral approach, and for your tremendous skill doing your job at an elite level. Thanks to you, Judith Curr, HarperOne, and HarperCollins for your willingness to believe in me.

Russell Wilson, thank you for the magical vision you laid out for yourself in my office in January of 2012. There was no way I was going to miss this ride! I'm so grateful for the opportunity to participate with you and the relevance you've given me. I love you and your incredible understanding of me as a human, and of my life's own unique challenges. Teaching this hasn't created an immunity, and you've never judged my struggles, and have always stood strong by my side. We both have much left to do with our individual careers, Limitless Minds, and much, much more. Ciara, you entered Russell's life and immediately helped all of us *Level Up*. I'm thankful for our relationship and for every conversation after game days on Sundays in the fall. You are a superstar in your own right and have been an incredible force-multiplier for the vision Russell shared with me in 2012. I have no doubts that the best is ahead.

Chad Bohling, you are the most caring, considerate, and kind-hearted person I have ever known. To me, you are the best in our industry, and you are a model of consistency. In the toughest times of my life your presence grows. Who does that? Not many. I can't thank you enough.

Mark Rodgers, I appreciate our every conversation more than you know. Your example as a husband, father, and agent continues to inspire me. You are one of the most impactful people I've ever met.

Mike Ryan, thank you for giving Chad and me a shot to work with Coach Coughlin and the Jacksonville Jaguars. It was you who believed in two twenty-plus-year-olds in advance of much efficacy or proof. Stay strong and continue your great work covering the NFL for NBC.

Fred Taylor, nine years' brother, the west official's locker room. Thank you for showing up every week and trusting Chad and me to "partner" with your mind, your behavior, your incredible talent, and your warrior spirit. You gave Jim Brown a run for his money. There is no book or career for me without you. I love everything you were and everything you've become.

Michael Johnson, you are and were the efficacy every great researcher is looking for in the field of human performance. Thank you for coming into my life, for allowing me to be a part of yours, and for the thousands of questions you've answered about scenarios, both hypothetical and real. You define world-class in everything you've ever done and continue to do.

Kaylee, you moved my soul at a time when I wasn't sure I had one. I don't know how you did it while humbling me in those very same moments, but it happened, and I needed it, and I will forever be indebted to you no matter which paths or directions life takes us. You are exceptional and remain one of the most engaging people I've ever met.

Alan Zucker, thank you for negotiating every element of this opportunity with HarperOne and for your steadfast vision and faith. You are a super-agent in the true sense of those words. Thank you for making me feel like Taylor, Danica, Deshaun, Joe, Timberlake, and the Mannings: your "real" clients! Truthfully, your belief helped me doubt my own doubt in myself. Thank you, Zuck.

George Pyne, you were eight direct reports above me running IMG, but you always treated me with so much humanity and appreciation for my nontraditional business skill set. That meant more than you know. To Helene, Brendan, Shannon, Drew, Jimmy, and Rachel, thanks to all of you for always allowing me to tag along with the Pyne family!

Nick Bollettieri, thank you for the evolution you led me on. I am so glad I went to work with you at IMG Academy. Mark Verstegen, Tom Durkin, John Ellinger, Loren Seagrave, Jose Lambert, Craig Friedman, Graeme Lauriston, Red Ayme, and the many incredible coaches I'd get to support in Bradenton, Florida, and Phoenix, Arizona—thanks to all of you for your openness and willingness to allow me to support your athletes and staff.

Tom Condon, Jeff Berry, Casey Close, Brodie Van Wagenen, Arnold Tarzy, Ken Kremer, Carlos Fleming, Max Eisenbud, Jimmy Sexton, Ed Marynowitz, and the amazing agents who live their lives in the background of the world's best performers, a special thanks to all of you for calling, teaching, educating, and trusting me in the moments in which the world seemed to be closing in far too fast on them, on you, and on us together. We always seemed to get through it.

Mom, Bob Jr., Grace, Bo, Diana, Mark, Vicky, Lisa, the Gilmers, the cousins and family in Seattle, Washington, thank you for always making me feel welcome when I'd get those rare moments to reengage in traditional life. I love you guys.

Coach Saban, thank you for the example you set, the class you live by, the programs you engineer, and the personal words you've shared with me in career changes, tough times, and after the loss of my father. You are an amazing man, and I'm better for every moment of time I got to spend with you.

Jimbo, it took a superhero to follow Coach Bowden and that's exactly what you are in my opinion. Thank you for your trust, unflinching support, and the toughness you modeled for me and so many others.

Kirby Smart, thank you for bringing me with you to Athens, Georgia. You embraced everything we learned together about the mind and the mission to stay neutral. You manage some of the most powerful pressures of the sports world, and you've embraced it as a privilege.

Mario, Mel, Locks, Coley, Ed, Billy D, Lawrence, Schmidty, Coch, JD, Sinclair, Doc, Colm, Newy, Gil, Nuge, Duncan, Hack, Feld, G, Joeg's, Phil, MK, and the many other coaches who change people's lives daily, including mine, thank you.

Jon Schultz, you and Taryn Morgan have been my combined business foundation for fifteen years. Tough job.

Thank you. Harrison Wilson, Alex Dachis, Bryan Donovan, and DJ Eidson, it is on us to find this next level with Limitless Minds.

Ben Sherwood, thank you for your strategic vision and support at a time when only someone at your rare air could provide it. Truly humbling.

Captain Tom Chaby, you are a friend, a hero, and a world-class leader. You brought me into a community that inspires all of us. Thank you for your trust and your continued friendship. "Whatever you have to do, just find an excuse to win." No one says it better than the SEALs. To Marcus, and the many others I've met through USASOC, the Honor Foundation, and the special operations community, thank you for everything.

Freddy Adu, what a ride. Let's add some new, great sentences to the comma that has been there far too long. It is time for you to take that next step on your amazing journey. I've never doubted that you have everything it takes.

Clint, Jozy, Eddie, Parkhurst, Spector, and the many US Soccer players I was able to support in my early years, there's not a day that goes by that I don't remember those moments. Clint, what a career. I'll never forget that moment at 3:45 a.m. EST at Derek Leader's house when you dropped that goal on South Korea. What a goal, bro. Thank you for the depth of our friendship.

The athletes, wow, where to start. High school, college, NFL, MLB, NBA, so many incredible stories I've heard and lessons I've learned. Challenges are always relative to the people who face them, whether you're thirteen and playing youth soccer or thirty-two and at the end of your professional tennis career. Thanks to all of you for allowing me to support you in your successes, and to help you navigate the inevitable challenges that living amongst the absolute best brings you.

Charles Wright Academy and Occidental College, I don't have enough words to thank you for helping raise me. You are special schools that have been led by special people. Thank you for everything.

Solange Marie, if I could go back and be a better version of myself in our time together, every day, every minute, every moment, I would. I'd do it so much better. But we don't get to live it again, so it's on both of us to find a new path forward. I've never relied more on neutral thinking than with this truth.

Lastly, to my father, thank you for the life you lived and the example you set for me. I love you. I close with one of your famous teachings. I don't think I've ever heard it said better.

"The best day of your life is the one on which you decide your life is your own. No apologies or excuses. No one to lean on, rely on, or blame. The gift is yours—it is an amazing journey—and you alone are responsible for the quality of it."

—Trevor Moawad

Notes

Chapter 1: It Takes Neutral Thinking

1 Russell Wilson, interview by Bryant Gumbel, *Real Sports*, HBO, April 21, 2015.

2 Wilson, *Real Sports*.

3 Jim Lovell, Apollo 13 post-flight press conference, NASA/JSC, 1970.

4 *Apollo 13 Technical Air-to-Ground Voice Transcription*, prepared by Test Division, Apollo Spacecraft Program Office, NASA (Houston, TX, April 1970), p. 411, https://www.hq.nasa.gov/office/pao/History/alsj/a13/AS13_TEC.PDF.

5 *Apollo 13 Technical Air-to-Ground Voice Transcription*, p. 411.

Chapter 2: It Takes a Plan

1 "Down in the Valley," track 4 on The Head and the Heart, *The Head and the Heart*, Sub Pop, 2011.

2 Charles F. Coleman Jr., "Ebony Goes off the Gridiron with Cam Newton," *Ebony*, April/May 2016.

Chapter 3: It Takes Hard Choices

1 Christopher Cason, "The Real-Life Diet of Vince Carter," *GQ*, April 5, 2017, https://www.gq.com/story/vince-carter-real-life-diet.

2 "LSU's Russell Puts on Impressive Show for Scouts," ESPN (website), March 15, 2007, https://www.espn.com/nfl/draft07/news/story?id= 2798856.

3 Tom Rinaldi, *JaMarcus Russell: Waking Up*, ESPN, April 22, 2013.

Chapter 4: It Takes a Verbal Governor

1 Baumeister et al., "Bad Is Stronger Than Good," *Review of General Psychology* 5, no. 4 (December 2001): 323–70, https://doi.org/10.1037 /1089-2680.5.4.323.

2 Metzger et al., "Worry Changes Decision Making: The Effect of Negative Thoughts on Cognitive Processing," *Journal of Clinical Psychology* 46, no. 1 (January 1990): 78–88, https://onlinelibrary.wiley .com/doi/abs/10.1002/1097-4679%28199001%2946%3A1%3C78%3A% 3AAID-JCLP2270460113%3E3.0.CO%3B2-R.

3 Andrew Parker, Alexandra Gerbasi, and Christine L. Porath, "The Effects of De-energizing Ties in Organizations and How to Manage Them," *Organizational Dynamics* 42, no. 2 (April–June 2013): 110–8, http://dx.doi.org/10.1016/j.orgdyn.2013.03.004.

4 Dunn et al., "Turning Gold into Lead: Dampening Appraisals Reduce Happiness and Pleasantness and Increase Sadness During Anticipation and Recall of Pleasant Activities in the Laboratory," *Behaviour Research and Therapy* 107 (August 2018): 19–33, https:// doi.org/10.1016/j.brat.2018.05.003.

5 William M. Kelley, Dylan D. Wagner, and Todd F. Heatherton, "In Search of a Human Self-Regulation System," *Annual Review of Neuroscience* 38 (July 2015): 389–411, https:/doi.org/10.1146/annurev -neuro-071013-014243.

6 Neuvonen et al., "Late-Life Cynical Distrust, Risk of Incident Dementia, and Mortality in a Population-Based Cohort," *Neurology* 82, no. 24 (June 2014): 2205–2212, https://doi.org/10.1212/WNL .0000000000000528.

7 Bill Buckner, interview by Don Shane, "Bill Buckner Talks Before World Series," WBZ-TV, October 6, 1986.

8 Associated Press, "Maravich Said in 1974: 'I Don't Want . . . to Die of a Heart Attack at Age 40,'" *Los Angeles Times,* January 7, 1988, https://www.latimes.com/archives/la-xpm-1988-01-07-sp-34024 -story.html.

9 Matthew McConaughey, "Matthew McConaughey to Grads: Always Play Like an Underdog," *TIME*, May 17, 2015, https://time.com /collection-post/3881954/matthew-mcconaughey-graduation-speech -university-of-houston.

10 *Cheers*, season 4, episode 18, "The Peterson Principle," directed by James Burrows, written by Glen Charles, Les Charles, James Burrows, Peter Casey, and David Lee, aired February 13, 1986, on NBC.

Chapter 6: It Takes an Ad Campaign in Your Brain

1 Price Pritchett, *Hard Optimism: How to Succeed in a World Where Positive Wins* (New York: McGraw-Hill, 2007).

2 Marcus Fairs, "Nike's 'Just Do It' Slogan Is Based on a Murderer's Last Words, Says Dan Wieden," *Dezeen*, March 14, 2015, https:// www.dezeen.com/2015/03/14/nike-just-do-it-slogan-last-words -murderer-gary-gilmore-dan-wieden-kennedy/.

3 Fairs, "Nike's 'Just Do It' Slogan."

Chapter 7: It Takes Visualizing

1 *The Matrix*, directed by Lana Wachowski and Lilly Wachowski (1999; Los Angeles, CA: Warner Bros.).

Chapter 8: It Takes Self-Awareness

1 Martin M. Broadwell, "Teaching for Learning (XVI.)," *The Gospel Guardian*, February 20, 1969, https://edbatista.typepad.com/files /teaching-for-learning-martin-broadwell-1969-conscious-competence -model.pdf.

2 Norman Vincent Peale, *The Power of Positive Thinking* (New York: Prentice-Hall, 1952).

Chapter 10: It Takes Leadership

1 LeBron James, "Finals All-Access: LeBron James and Draymond Green Mic'd Up," NBA, June 4, 2015, https://www.youtube.com /watch?v=8d6NsAXI0uY.

2 Tim Cook, "Tim Cook: 'Be Fearless,' Duke University Commencement 2018 Speech," Duke University, May 13, 2018, https://www.youtube .com/watch?v=Jr4LC1q1N_g, 6:50.

3 Joseph Tsai, "Alibaba Group's Joe Tsai Talks Pac-12 China," Alibaba Group, September 10, 2015, https://www.youtube.com/watch?v=AcrTgel073g&t=102s, 0:48.

4 Tony Blair, "Tony Blair Addresses the Yale College Class of 2008," Yale University, May 26, 2008, https://www.youtube.com/watch?v=Q6F6iGNpQX0&t=6s, 12:12.

Chapter 12: It Takes What It Takes

1 "Justice Grinds Slow; Man Wants Back in Jail," *The News Tribune* (Tacoma, WA), September 4, 1975.

About the Author

Trevor Moawad, president of Moawad Consulting Group and CEO and cofounder of Limitless Minds, is a mental conditioning coach to elite performers. He has worked closely with prestigious NCAA football programs and coaches and been part of eight national championship games. Additionally, Moawad has supported the US special operations community, Major League Baseball, the NBA, UFC, and many other elite professionals. He has been featured in both sports and mainstream media, including *Sports Illustrated*, *USA Today*, ESPN, Fox Sports, and NPR. He lives in Scottsdale, Arizona.

Andy Staples covers college football for *The Athletic*. He also hosts *Playbook* weekdays on SiriusXM Channel 84. He covered college football for *Sports Illustrated* from 2008 to 2019.